Liturgical Life Principles

Liturgical Life Principles

How Episcopal Worship Can Lead to
Healthy and Authentic Living

IAN S. MARKHAM

MOREHOUSE PUBLISHING

an imprint of
Church Publishing Incorporated
New York   Harrisburg

Morehouse Publishing, 4775 Linglestown Road, Harrisburg, PA 17112
Morehouse Publishing, 445 Fifth Avenue, New York, NY 10016

Morehouse Publishing is an imprint of Church Publishing Incorporated.

Cover design by Corey Kent
Interior design by John Eagleson

Library of Congress Cataloging-in-Publication Data

Markham, Ian S.
    Liturgical life principles : how Episcopal worship can lead to healthy and authentic living / by Ian S. Markham.
        p. cm.
    Includes bibliographical references.
    ISBN 978-0-8192-2324-1 (pbk.)
    1. Public worship – Episcopal Church. I. Title.
BX5940.M27 2009
264'.03 – dc22

                                                        2008043057

Printed in the United States of America

09   10   11   12   13   14   10   9   8   7   6   5   4   3   2   1

To my father and stepmother,
For the witness to the faith, thank you

Contents

Acknowledgments

Perhaps the greatest joy of joining the community at Virginia Theological Seminary comes from its practice of daily corporate worship. Three times a day there is a service in the chapel — Morning Prayer, Eucharist, and Evening Prayer. Like countless students and faculty before me, I have come to develop a deep appreciation for the beauty of the Book of Common Prayer. The richness of the prose and the elegance of the service structure are remarkable.

So the greatest debt I owe in writing this book is to the entire VTS community. Already I am learning much from faculty colleagues and students. For their presence in our shared worship life I am deeply grateful.

I have tried to keep endnotes to a minimum, but I would like to express certain intellectual debts. For an appreciation of the connection between liturgy and life I am grateful to Charles Price and Louis Weil and their book *Liturgy for Living* (Seabury Press, 1979). For much of the theology permeating the book I continue to be grateful to the work of Keith Ward, in particular his book *Divine Action* (Collins, 1990).

Along the way I asked friends to look at sections. Bob Prichard at Virginia Theological Seminary answered some of my questions. Bill Roberts checked the chapter on music in the service. Mitzi Budde, the director of the library, tracked down some important texts for me. I am very grateful to Robin Gulick, Barney Hawkins, Betsy Baumgarten, Oran Warder, and Amy Dyer, who read the manuscript and offered feedback in discussion.

To write a book while serving as dean and president is difficult. It is possible only because of the exceptional team around me. I am grateful therefore to Katie Lasseron, Tim Sedgwick, Amy Dyer, Roger Ferlo, Barney Hawkins, Marge McNaughton, and Heather Zdancewicz. I am also grateful to the recently retired Ed Hall.

I continue to be deeply grateful to my lovely wife, Lesley, and my amazing son, Luke.

I am grateful to the team at Church Publishing, especially to Davis Perkins, with whose help, at a stimulating breakfast, I sketched out the shape of this book.

I was especially interested in the response of my father. Keith Markham and my stepmother, Shireen, are both Baptists who find the world of Anglicanism a little strange. So I am grateful that they read the manuscript, and I am even more grateful that they seem to appreciate it. I dedicate this book to them with all my love.

Introduction

Seven hundred years ago in Europe, most people did not travel more than ten miles from the place of their birth during their entire lifetime. Most people worked on the land. They would marry, raise children, and die in close proximity to their entire extended family. Generations came and went, yet this basic pattern of life endured for centuries.

Life in modern America could not be more different. Urban life has emerged with its paradox that millions live in close proximity, but relationships are often transient. Employment requires mobility, which means children may be raised thousands of miles away from grandparents. Endless retraining is required: the world is changing rapidly, and all of us find our skill sets need to be updated. Job security is rare. Globalization has seen certain types of employment go overseas. Although there are many advantages to the modern age (for example, dentistry, hygiene, and communication), there are particular stresses that our forebears did not have to handle.

Every moment in history has its problems, and our post-9/11 world is no exception. We board the aircraft worried about the suicide bomber. The thriller movie has replaced the Russian enemy with the terrorist who acquires a nuclear weapon from a rogue state. We are accustomed to worrying about natural disasters (too much snow, rain, or wind), but now we must deal with the avian flu, not to mention global warming and rising sea levels that threaten to make parts of America uninhabitable. Sustainability of our modern lifestyle appears unlikely as we watch India and China make increasing demands on the finite supplies of oil. We can add to all this the normal worries of living — making sure our children avoid drugs, affording health care as we grow old, and staying married.

Ah, yes — staying married! So we come to the complicated world of sex. Americans are in a real muddle about sex. On a typical night in America, half of the occupants in our business hotels are watching an adult movie.[1] Some 45–55 percent of women and 55–65 percent of men have had an affair at some point in their life.[2] And of course, the Internet has opened up all sorts of possibilities. We now talk about "cyber infidelity." Some marriages absorb a certain ambiguity of practice and behavior, but others do not. The result is divorce, and with divorce often come economic stress, loneliness, bitterness, and alienated children.

Perhaps it is because we are sexual beings that we find ourselves deeply preoccupied with appearances. I am forty-five years old. My waistline is getting larger, my hairline is receding, and signs of aging are appearing everywhere. Commercials constantly exhort us to look different, so we end up constantly anxious. Most of us are unhappy with some aspect of our physical makeup. We commit to the latest fad diet or purchase the exercise machine, which never gets used.

It can be difficult to cope. As a result, we are all searching. Sales of self-help books are booming; health spas are thriving; the therapist and counselor are in demand; and some resort to a "cult" or a "spiritual" movement.

While the self-help books, the therapists, and the various spiritual movements can be helpful, my claim in this book is that there is a better place to go. The whole purpose of the Christian liturgy is to provide the resources to enable God to facilitate healthy and authentic living — healthy in mind, body, and spirit and authentic in recognizing the realities of being a mortal creature in this world. The purpose of the worship of God is to help us see our dependence on God and the vast resources that God wants to lavish on our lives. *The healthy and authentic living project* has to do with worshiping God in the Episcopal liturgy. This phrase needs some explaining.

Through worship, God invites us to work on a lifetime project — a project that will require considerable time but generate enormous benefits. This project captures our reason for being. And the argument of this book is that the Episcopal liturgy provides both health and authenticity. Health requires a positive outlook for living in the world, which we definitely find in the Episcopal liturgy. However, this project is larger: it also invites authenticity. The point here is that a healthy disposition need not be authentic. We can contrive to be positive when we need to be angry. We can refuse to dig down and examine the triggers that make situations difficult. Most of us have places where we have been damaged, which are often the places that make us damaging to others. When something trivial becomes major, a button has been pushed that needs attention. Authenticity requires that we go there.

The argument of this book is that authenticity should underpin and sustain the healthy disposition. And authenticity can create many paradoxes. It is authentic to live life aware of the inevitability of death. Thus, when illness strikes one can have a healthy attitude toward that illness. Because of the centrality of the Holy Communion, the connection between life and death is inescapable in the Episcopal liturgy, enabling us to cultivate both a *healthy* and *authentic* approach to life.

As we work through the liturgy, we shall discover that the resources to create this disposition are grounded in the work of the Holy Spirit, revealed in the Word, and enabled by the Creator. The resources of the liturgy are found in many traditions — including especially Roman Catholic, Lutheran, and Orthodox — but this book is going to concentrate on the Book of Common Prayer as it has been developed by the Episcopal Church.

Indeed our focus will be even more limited. This book is a reading of the service of Holy Eucharist (Rite 2, the service most commonly used on Sunday mornings) in terms of equipping us to live healthy and authentic lives — with our worries in check and our values appropriately sorted. Toward the end of the book, I touch on the services of Morning and Evening Prayer. Really effective living requires time each day with God.

My claim will strike some readers as bizarre. Is it really possible that these uncomfortable pews in drafty churches — where people all read from a script — and it isn't obvious when to stand or sit — could be a resource for healthy living?

In this book I hope to show that the answer is yes. However, healthy living does not come easily. It requires the constant weekly discipline of allowing the liturgy to penetrate and change us from the inside out. Appreciating the liturgy does require work, but learning to interpret the words, actions, and movement of the liturgy enables them to be vehicles for the transforming power of God.

All Episcopal congregations are not the same. Most of the parts of the service described in this book occur in most Episcopal churches. Some, however, carry out parts differently; some don't include every part, and some introduce other parts that I don't discuss.

However, the book does describe a fairly typical experience that you should recognize if you find yourself in an Episcopal church.

This book is written for those interested in the Episcopal Church. Perhaps you have visited an Episcopal church once and are thinking of going again. Perhaps you are in a class for Adult Enquirers. Although the book could be adapted for teenagers, the primary focus is for adults who are trying to cope with the stresses and demands of living in modern America. I have attempted to keep technical language to a minimum and to explain it when it is used. However, I am hoping that lifelong Episcopalians might appreciate the study — those who want to fall in love again with the liturgy.

Perhaps the easiest way to engage the book is to read it from beginning to end, which should provide an overview of the impact of participating in the worship of God through the Episcopal liturgy. However, it can also be read more slowly. At the end of each *Liturgical Life Principle* (an important life-enhancing principle that is the key point of a particular part of the liturgy), there is a suggestion for meditation. The idea is to read from the book before the service and focus on a particular section, with its Liturgical Life Principle, and use the meditation during the service.

The goal is to discover the rich resources that God is making available to transform us into the people whom God wants us to be. God wants to do the work: we need to let God do the work. Participating fully in the liturgy of the Episcopal Church is a rich way to let God transform us all.

The first chapter is a sketch of the divine transformation that God wants to work in all our lives. It constantly refers to LLPs (Liturgical Life Principles), which are described later in the book. The idea is this: the project — this life task — of a transformed life, where love is at the center, is made possible when a person worships God in the liturgy. In chapter 1, I describe the life that God intends us to live: the transformed life. When you have finished the book, you can go back to the references in this chapter to the different parts of the liturgy and how they relate to the various aspects of a transformed life.

Chapter One

What Does the Healthy and Authentic Living Project Look Like?

Being human can be complicated. We mess up so easily. Christianity explains both why we mess up and offers a vision of how we are intended to be. Christians believe that there is a way that we are intended to be. The whole concept of a "healthy and authentic living project" assumes that humans should live in a certain way. Unpacking this assumption is the purpose of this chapter.

The Spiritual Foundation

For the Christian, there is no question. The starting place for healthy and authentic living is in the recognition that we are connected with the Divine. A key assumption of this study is that God is really there. God made us. We are living in a universe that God intended. This vast cosmos wanted human lives to emerge. Fortunately, thanks to discoveries in modern physics this idea doesn't sound as outlandish as it once did. Physicists are very sensitive to the remarkable maths that made the universe possible. Indeed some talk about the anthropic principle: that the probability of the universe being so finely tuned to enable us to emerge is so high that it looks fixed. It looks like this universe was always intended for planets that can sustain life to emerge. And it is remarkable that all the factors came together. It could have so easily been different: all the odds pointed to a chaotic universe in which life would have been impossible. But instead of the likely, we have the highly unlikely. Order emerged out of the potential chaos. Of course, it might just be a giant fluke. However, Christians would want to say that intention and purpose were at work in this universe. God wanted creatures who had the capacity to receive and give love.

The goal of living is that we discover the gift of love. We are intended to be born into families — with parents who teach us how to give and receive love. We are intended to grow into adults and seize those moments when we can create deep, committed relationships with others around us. And most important of all, we are intended to recognize that God loves us, that God desires to surround us with love and peace. It important for us to recognize that God desperately wants to facilitate an appropriate orientation toward love (Liturgical Life Principle 2 — henceforth LLP), and God wants to be involved in all our endeavors (LLP 4). (Here we have two references to parts of the liturgy that will be examined in more detail below.)

Once this is recognized, then we can see why the underlying disposition to life should be one of gratitude (LLP 24). This perhaps is the fundamental divide between the person of faith and the person who cannot see God. The person of faith is in a state of perpetual gratitude. Every morning we wake up: miracle number one for the day. Every day we have a body that operates effectively (and, hopefully, most of the time): miracle number two for the day. Every day we notice the dew in the grass, the sun rising, and the beauty of the flower: miracle number three for the day. And so on. If we are surrounded by so many moments of divine grace, we find ourselves perpetually grateful — grateful to God for the miracle of this day.

If we look at the world through the lenses of gratitude, then life is so much more delightful. It creates a sense of joy that cannot help but be healthy. However, this gratitude is not simply for the great gift of being, but also for what we believe God has done for us.

Thus far a person of any faith tradition could affirm the above account. However, faith traditions diverge about precisely what God has done and is doing in the world. We are not just affirming some nebulous "spiritual force" that permeates the universe. This God has told us what he (or she, because of course God is beyond gender) is like.

The revelation of God for Christians is a life. Contrary to the popular perception, the primary Word of God is the life, death, and resurrection of a person — namely, Jesus of Nazareth. All Christian theology is in the business of reading this life. When we ask the obvious question, "How do we know what God is like?" the answer is, "We read what God is like in the life, death, and resurrection of Jesus." How do I know that God is loving and identifies with those who are suffering? Because I can see this in the words and deeds —

to quote Acts 1 — of Jesus of Nazareth. How do I know that God understands our pain? Because I can see this in the death and suffering of Jesus. How do I know that God understands vulnerability? Because God was vulnerable as a babe in a manger. Knowledge of God is grounded in the revelation of God, which is supremely found in Jesus.

This means that it is vitally important to read and study Scripture, for it is in the written word that we learn about the Eternal Word. Consequently, this project highlights the obligation to learn what God is like through Scripture (see LLP 6, 7, and 23). As a result of learning about the nature of God, we find ourselves with a heightened sense of gratitude, for this God is a God of consistent love.

This is the foundation for the healthy and authentic living project. The project is grounded in a claim about the nature of the world: it is not a freak phenomenon but an entity created by a God who intended each and every one of us.

Objective Morality

Once we recognize that God exists and that we need to be in conversation with God, the next stage follows logically. The purpose of worship is to acknowledge the appropriate value of everything. When we bow the knee and see in God the fullness of love, beauty, and justice, we start to see the standards by which everything should be judged. Morality for the Christian is not determined by culture or individuals. There is not "a right for me and a different right for you." If this were the case then the Nazi anti-Semitic morality would be on a par with the morality of Nelson Mandela's antiapartheid morality. Christians reject this. Instead morality is grounded in the nature of God. Therefore, worship of God is vitally important in the healthy and authentic living project. It is in worship that we recognize what matters (LLP 3); it is in prayer that we locate our, often very local, worries (LLP 8). And it is vitally important to constantly affirm the divine values (LLP 26).

As a result of the constant, steady worship of God, we find our lives changing. We find that we instinctively know what is right and wrong. Even when the moral situation is complex, we are clearer about those actions at the extreme that would be morally unacceptable. We learn to distinguish with some clarity between actions that are truly life-enhancing and those that are not. It is so easy to deceive ourselves. We can easily imagine that this pornographic Internet website or that opportunity to pad our expenses can be justified. And the act of sitting in the presence of God makes one realize the error of these deceptions.

Dealing with Things

In worship we begin to order our values. Ordering our values can be difficult because the Gospel poses a major challenge. Repeatedly in the Gospels we are exhorted to be very careful with things. Indeed Jesus instructs the rich to give to the poor and warns that it is harder for the rich man to get into the kingdom of God than for a "camel to get through the eye of a needle."

The point of Jesus' teaching is that things can easily become an obsession. We can get addicted. We become desperate to "shop until we drop," thereby accumulating even more possessions that we don't get around to enjoying or using. Possessions can end up distorting our lives. We start imagining that the imported vase is more important than the hungry child. And tragically, we can easily damage our relationship with the child as a result of investing so much "love" into the vase. The less stuff we have, explains Jesus, the more likely we will focus on the things that really matter. So it is important that the healthy and authentic living project recognize the danger of things (LLP 11).

Dealing with the Past

When we are young, life is uncomplicated. We know what is right and wrong. We have ideals; we still believe in uncomplicated romantic love — meeting the right person and settling down. As we become adults life becomes much more complicated. Our ideals are compromised by the demands of modern living; many discover that romantic love doesn't survive day-to-day living; and many of us have behaved in ways that we deeply regret.

Christians believe that God has dealt decisively with the past. God has absorbed our past into the act of God in Christ. God has the authority to forgive us. We can offer the past back to God knowing that the death of Christ on the cross has made all the difference. This is most important for healthy living. The past can so easily haunt us. It is difficult to escape the tentacles of the past, for the past can reach out and destroy the present. So many individuals repeat the mistakes of the past: the woman who escapes one abusive husband only to marry another or the person who was neglected as a child and who goes on to neglect his own children. And even if our experience isn't that dramatic, we often allow the past to destroy the quality of the present. Sometimes it is just the painful memories; for others it is the inability to commit to the possibilities of the present. We are all exhorted to give our past to God.

In giving God the past, we are freed up to enjoy the present. Often the consequences of the past will still have to be tolerated, but the power of the past is eliminated. We are invited to enjoy the work that God has done in Christ. Liturgically, this work is done in two places. During the exchange of the "peace of Lord," we should allow the peace of God to transform our relationships with everyone (both present and past) (LLP 10). And again during the postcommunion prayer, we give to God all this hard work of coping with our past (LLP 22).

The following picture of a healthy person is emerging. This is a person who recognizes the necessity of being connected to the Being that enables us to be. The heart of that recognition is the act of worship, which enables us to recognize those values that matter most. As we worship we sort out our priorities. Among those priorities is the imperative of not allowing "things" — that big car, antique vase, and plasma television — to distort the really important aspects of our life, namely, our relationships with people. In dealing with people, life can become very complicated. And sometimes we find ourselves harboring regret and hurt as a result of mixed and complicated encounters with each other. We have just seen how important it is to offer the past to God. However, in offering the past to God it is important to make sure that our relationships with others in the present are healthy and positive. It is to the struggles in the present that we now turn.

Coping with the Inevitable Struggles

Having dealt with the past, we can now concentrate on the present. Christians have no delusions about people. We are not simply muddled, confused, and often morally ambiguous. We also have the capacity to be selfish, unkind, cruel, inconsiderate, self-absorbed, and sometimes downright wicked. This is all captured by the very simple and prosaic word "sin."

At one level, sin is puzzling. Why do we opt for destruction and hatred rather than building love? Why do we ruin a happy marriage by a one-night stand? Why do we jeopardize a successful career by cheating on our expenses? Why do people choose to torture, rape, and kill rather than enjoy the beauty of creation and the love of others? It seems utterly irrational.

At another level, sin is often seen as a calculated risk. We suspect that we can "get away with it," that we will be undetected. Alternatively, we imagine that our power will protect us. As a result, egoism, stupidity, and a delight in cruelty are deeply embedded in each and every one of us. Egoism wants it all: the happy marriage, the public face, and the rendezvous with a lover. Egoism flirts with the illusion that somehow the regular rules do not apply to us. We lie to ourselves. We tell ourselves that we are not really destroying our inner integrity by this act of betrayal. Stupidity is seen in the belief that we will get away with "it" and the accumulation of lies once we are detected. We are stupid when we take a risk with everything that is precious to us for the sake of an evening of lust or a less than accurate tax return. And the delight in cruelty is a discovery made by the young, who can mercilessly tease the weaker, smaller, different child. There is a perverse delight and satisfaction that can be found in hatred and dislike. We like the bonding it creates with the group. We unleash pain on others. And perhaps it is only much later that we regret the hurt we have caused.

Sin is not simply a problem with actions. We are not good at recognizing the link between actions and our internal life. Our decision to find a pornography website feeds the imagination. Then we are tempted to live out the fantasy. The desperate quest for power, lived out in an elaborate fantasy of the exercise of power, can lead to destructive friendships and abuse of relationships. The insatiable quest for a new car, where we pore over the magazines and covet the car every time we see it, can lead to fiscal irregularities. Normally our negative actions are an expression of an undisciplined internal life. Jesus saw this clearly. The Sermon on the Mount (Matt. 5–7) teaches that it is important to control not simply actions but also the internal life that underpins actions.

The goal is to create habits so that we no longer run the risks of sin. We want to become vehicles that radiate the love of God. We don't simply want to be able to turn down opportunities for sin; we want to become people who don't want to sin. This goal will take some time to reach, and this is where the liturgical approach to healthy and authentic living comes very much into its own.

The liturgy is constructed in such a way that we will sit through a service saying the general confession and then come back next week and say it all over again. Overcoming our propensities toward sin will take some time (LLP 9). God is deeply aware of the human inclination to praise God one day and behave in ways that are deeply distorted the next (LLP 14). When we turn to God, God becomes a partner in the work of transformation; we are not alone in our struggles (LLP 21). And it is often through music and meditation that we can work through our struggles (LLP 33).

God's willingness to be there for us is the most precious gift of all. We are not doing this work alone. God is there, willing and ready to help us with it all.

Offering God the Details of Our Life

Most books that encourage a changed outlook on life are known as self-help books (so called because we are required to do the work). The liturgical approach to the healthy and authentic living project makes this a God-help book. God is love. God understands the challenges involved in becoming vehicles for love. And God has done everything to make love a possibility in our lives.

When we think of worshiping God, it is important not to turn God into a big person. God is not a giant ego in the sky to whom we pander by saying nice things. However, when we think about God and the muddles of our life, it is entirely appropriate to see God as our cosmic friend (LLP 28). God is ready and willing to walk with us. We are never alone. However difficult life can become, God is present in the difficulties. This does not mean that everything will be smooth. The primary New Testament image for discipleship is "taking up a cross" (a willingness to be martyred). Right from the start, Christianity teaches a God who is alongside us in our pain and suffering, not a God who will eliminate our pain and suffering.

While we recognize the inevitability of pain and suffering in life, we are constantly invited to offer to God all the details of our life. Our concerns, fears, and aspirations are all offered to God. Parents should offer to God their daily worry about their children;

children can offer to God their hopes for career and romance. We are constantly surrounded by a cosmic being who wants to uphold us (LLP 24). This God of the details promises to attend to and be present in those details.

Drawing on the Resource of the Sacrament

Christians believe that God has provided a distinctive precious resource that can really make a difference: the Holy Eucharist. Along with baptism, this is the defining practice of a Christian. The climax of the second half of weekly Episcopalian worship is the Holy Eucharist.

Christians believe that this is a gift left to the church by Jesus himself. The act of participation takes us across the centuries to the eve of the day when Jesus was betrayed. We also believe that there is real power in the prayer uttered by the priest over the bread and wine. The Eternal Word present in Jesus is present also in the elements we receive. They become more than just bread and wine. They are to us "the body and blood of our Lord."

While our state of mind is important when we take the sacrament, the effectiveness of the sacrament does not depend on that state of mind. It has a power that is way beyond our attitude. It is a resource that makes a difference (LLP 17). The act of receiving the Eucharist helps us live differently.

The practice of the early Christians in Jerusalem was to "break the bread daily." Tragically, a distorted view of the sacraments emerged in the history of the church, and there were countless generations who never received the sacrament. It has been a liturgical struggle to bring the sacrament back to the place it had in the early church. Recognizing this, we should value the opportunity to take the Holy Eucharist at least once a week (LLP 30, 31).

The act of remembering God dying is a powerful act on many levels. It isn't simply remembering the act of love embodied in Christ; it is also a reminder that suffering is part of the human condition. To suffering, we turn next.

Coping with Suffering

It is often said that the major challenge to faith is the problem of suffering. Much is made of the apparent contradiction: if God is all-powerful, then God must be able to abolish suffering; if God is all-loving, then God must wish to abolish suffering. But suffering exists; therefore God cannot be all-powerful and all-loving. From the outside, it looks self-contradictory: the belief in God (as traditionally understood) is incompatible with the reality of suffering and evil in the world.

Normally, advocates of a worldview do not like to dwell on the aspects of that worldview that others find most problematic. If you are a politician, for example, you stress the aspects of your program that people find most attractive and play down those aspects that people find problematic. However, when it comes to Christianity and suffering, Christians make suffering central to their faith.

Our Scriptures are dominated by the theme of suffering. And liturgically the reality of suffering is placed front and center. A cross is carried at the front of the procession into church (LLP 1). The death of Jesus is remembered in the Eucharist. But nowhere in the Bible is suffering explained. Instead the Christian response to suffering is to recognize God in Christ hanging on the cross.

This is a powerful response. Although we do not know precisely why suffering is tolerated within creation, we do know that God participates in our suffering. This would imply that whatever the reason for suffering, it must be a good reason. Even God could not escape the grip of suffering.

On Good Friday we see the full participation of God in suffering, God's identification with all those who suffer. It is a revelatory act: we learn that God is with all those who are being tortured, humiliated, who are coping with loss and pain. On Easter Sunday, we see the promise of God's triumph over suffering. We see the hope of the resurrection, which, as St. Paul explains, is an anticipation of what all creation will ultimately enter (Rom. 8).

Christians do not deny the reality of suffering. There is no promise in Scripture of a suffering-free life. Such a promise would be absurd. We all know that this life ends in death. And we also know that death is associated with suffering. Christians are invited to recognize and live into this reality. Responding to this invitation is part of living authentically. We do not delude ourselves. Life is fragile; living is a precious gift. We know that it will not go on forever.

When we live liturgically, we find ourselves bringing our own suffering and the suffering of others constantly to God. We find ourselves pleading for divine intervention to make a difference (LLP 8).

As we will see in chapter 3, sometimes God is able to use the avenues opened by prayer to create some space for healing; at other times, for reasons that are inevitably beyond us, it looks like that is not an option for God. This is because God is working within the rules that God has set within creation. God is not going to suddenly override the structures of creation. To stop the stray bullet from killing the child might well involve a structural violation of creation that would make responsibility within creation impossible.

I was seventeen when my mother died. I remember vividly my feelings of rage and anger directed to God (and pretty much everyone else around me). These feelings are perfectly appropriate. Indeed we are invited to rage at God — this is the witness of the Psalms. For about two weeks I declared to the world that I was an atheist. Then a wise old man named Mr. Foster, who was counseling me, just paused and stared at me during one of my rants and said: "Ian, didn't you realize before this moment that others have lost their mother? Didn't you know that Jesus himself was taken from those who loved him while still a relatively young man?"

The point is simple: this world is tragic. Every day a child dies; every day a mother is taken from a family; every day a good person is the victim of some deadly disease or evil act. The liturgical response is to recognize the centrality of suffering in our lives. We recognize the participation of God in that suffering (LLP 15). And we trust that God will ultimately transform suffering (LLP 16).

Suffering still hurts. To lose someone we love (especially a child) is completely devastating. Part of our weekly experience should be a meditation on the nature and awfulness of suffering. The focus is the crucifixion. It teaches us to appreciate those moments when we and those we love are well; it also prepares us for the reality of living in this world.

Facing Death Constructively

As with suffering, so with death. The healthy and authentic living project accepts the ultimate reality of death. As Paul notes in Romans 8, nothing can separate us from the love of God in Christ. I am forty-five; I hope to live a long life and be blessed to see my son grow up and form his own family. However, I also know that through Christ I have been granted the gift of what matters. Some people die young, and it's perfectly possible that I might be one of them.

So I live life in the light of death. I live aware of the fragile nature of existence. I appreciate every day that God has given me. I don't allow "things" to distort my vision of what matters. I recognize the supreme value of time spent with family, friends, and colleagues. I work hard to ensure that there isn't a continuing argument damaging my relationship with others. Many lives are deeply damaged because people allow an argument to remain unsettled, which then can never be settled because death intervenes. We should also make sure that those we love know we love them before they walk out the door. It is always possible that moment might be the last opportunity for significant communication. Ensuring that we communicate our deepest feelings to others is an important aspect of authentic living.

It is not morbid to live life in the light of death. Death should be recognized as a reality that shapes our living. As we have already observed, it should ensure that we live life with gratitude. It should ensure that we do not let our values be distorted by a needless preoccupation with things that ultimately do not matter. And finally, as Simeon discovered (LLP 27), we believe that in our encounter with Christ we do not have to fear death.

Comprehensive Year-Round Project

Slowly the picture of the healthy and authentic living project is emerging. It is a rich picture of a life that is balanced, well-adjusted, with priorities recognized, with values grounded in the character of God, and with an appropriate sensitivity to suffering and death. At this point, the author has a confession to make. Like most priests, I am still very much on this journey. I can see what God wants to do; I can also see how far I have to go.

And this is all okay as well. The joy of the liturgical approach is that we are invited to take our time. This is not an overnight procedure. We are going to take one day at a time. We are going to come back Sunday after Sunday and ask God to work on our lives. We are going to enter into the rich demands of the liturgical calendar (LLP 5). Each year, Lent is yet another opportunity to reflect on our progress and delve deeper into our contradictory, sinful personalities. Each day is yet another opportunity to acknowledge our failings before God and enjoy God's forgiveness. When we struggle, we might turn to music to inspire us (LLP 32). We might meditate on a symbol to help us (LLP 34).

We also take great comfort in the stories of all those who have gone before us. God has faced the problems in my life before. God has worked on transforming other lives. They are examples and an inspiration to us (LLP 13 and 30).

It is important not to rush this project. It is not simply a matter of reading this book and going to a Eucharist once. We need to commit to the journey. We need to be in constant conversation with the redeeming power of God's grace. We need to come back time and time again and let God do the work.

Being Transformed

Although the journey will be lifelong, it is also remarkable how rapidly God makes a difference. As we start allowing God to work through us in the liturgy, change will be seen. We will start praying as God intended (LLP 18); our priorities will be less distorted, and our inner disposition transformed. Living life with a disposition of gratitude instead of constant resentment is life-changing. Family and friends will enjoy the new positive you. Making sure that every parting moment is an opportunity to express love for those closest to us guarantees a sense of security in the knowledge of intimate love that makes all the difference.

So we start clarifying values. The paradox is that as we start to achieve balance we find more areas to work on. And often this means that the progress is not measured or celebrated. In one sense this is right and proper since we don't want to take pride in becoming holy. However, for those close to us the difference is clear. And for them we become a precious gift in their lives.

In the rest of the book we will look at how the liturgy is one of the divine mechanisms for bringing about change in our lives.

Chapter Two

Appreciating Liturgy

To appreciate anything takes some effort. For me as an Englishman, the world's greatest sport is football. It is played almost everywhere, partly because to play all you need is a ball and your feet. It can be played by street children in Brazil and by women in Germany; it can be played by the rich or the poor. It is the world's truly universal game.

When I arrived in the United States, I had to get used to the word "football" having a different meaning. Here it involves men dressed in padded armor, charging at each other, with a ball being thrown around a field. It looks like the English game of rugby. The game is constantly interrupted (mainly, it seems, for the ubiquitous American television commercial). From the outside it looked very odd.

And then I started on the journey. It began with the Super Bowl — the great American ritual when families and friends gather to enjoy the passion and energy of American football. Slowly I started to appreciate the strength and speed of these men as they slammed into each other. I started to appreciate the pauses in the game as the space to think through the options for each team during the next play. I started to learn the vocabulary — the blitz, end zone, and fumble. I read about Walter Camp (the father of American football) and Amos Alonzo Stagg (inventor of the "Statue of Liberty" play). I began to appreciate the rules and practices of this remarkable game from the inside.

Or to take another illustration. The appreciation of art takes some time. We need some knowledge to understand why great art is great. We need to know about the different periods in art history. To understand the genius of Michelangelo, we need to know a little about the Renaissance. The Italian rebirth (the literal meaning of "renaissance") challenged the stylized figures of medieval art and replaced them with warm, vibrant, beautiful people (often naked) in a way that really connects. Michelangelo received his great commission from Pope Julius II (which Michelangelo accepted only reluctantly since he saw himself as a sculptor). He then painted "The Creation of Adam" in the Sistine Chapel. In the countless pictures that I have seen of it (sadly I haven't yet made the journey to Rome to see the original), it is always breathtaking. It is not surprising that Michelangelo was described as "divine" as his art was revealed. A little knowledge of the period makes it possible to really appreciate the achievement. Unless we get inside, we don't begin to see what is really going on.

In almost any area of life, true appreciation requires learning. We need to learn the discourse of the area we are seeking to appreciate: the vocabulary, key concepts, and expressions that describe the details of the area. We must find some way of standing with people who appreciate the area and learning from them.

In the same way that I needed to give American football a chance and simply tune in and appreciate what others were seeing, so we need to give the liturgy the same chance. And just as it would have been insufficient for me simply to watch one football game by myself, so the appreciation of liturgy requires several trips to a church. We need to get used to the occasion. C. S. Lewis makes the point well when he explains why worshipers go to church:

> They go to *use* the service, or, if you prefer, to *enact* it. Every service is a structure of acts and words through which we receive a sacrament, or repent, or supplicate, or adore. And it enables us to do these things best — if you like, it "works" best — when, through long familiarity, we don't have to think about it. As long as you notice, and have to count, the steps, you are not yet dancing but only learning to dance. A good shoe is a shoe you don't notice. Good reading becomes possible when you need not consciously think about eyes, or light, or print, or spelling. The perfect church service would be one we were almost unaware of; our attention would have been on God.[3]

Appreciation requires time and energy: it takes time to understand the church year, the colors, the movement of the service, and the transforming expectations of the sacrament.

In the same way that there are bad football games, so there are disappointing church services. Sometimes the service can feel a little like "low-grade entertainment."[4] The music and singing are disappointing, the preaching is too long and incoherent, and the seating is uncomfortable. Those of us involved in the worship of God have an obligation to work at it with the best of our ability. Liturgy is work; etymologically it is literally the "work of the people." It is a labor that requires preparation and commitment. Services should be put together well.

Some of the strongest congregations in the country are the non-denominational megachurches, which provide high-tech concerts, with excellent contemporary praise music and preaching. It is the Disney of religion. There is a "show" feel: one is part of an audience. The Episcopal Church is more like a Smithsonian museum: it requires more effort and perhaps is less fun, but we learn more about how we relate to the world. In this service, one is a participant. There is work to do. There is at least one book to juggle, sometimes two or three. One must be willing to learn the conventions of the community — when to stand and sit. Like at the Smithsonian, we have to put some effort into the act of appreciating the occasion. However, also like at the Smithsonian, the benefit from such effort can be life-transforming.

So this is an invitation to give the liturgical tradition of the Episcopal Church a chance. It is an opportunity to discover the way the liturgy has been a vehicle of God's grace for countless lives. The focus is on the Episcopal Church; however, Anglicans everywhere will recognize the liturgical moments that are described. And of course the other great liturgical traditions — the Roman Catholics and the Lutherans in particular — will find much that resonates. Nevertheless, an Episcopal setting is assumed, and, with that setting, an understanding that God encounters us in different places on our faith journey. Episcopalians accept that not everyone is where I am. In fact I haven't always been where this book now is.

So we start the journey into understanding the Episcopal liturgy and discovering how it "works." The power of the liturgy resides in its capacity to converse with the complexity of our lives. The flow and movement provide space for worship, learning, confession, peace, and, finally, receiving the power of Christ through the sacrament into our lives. All this is examined and explored in subsequent chapters.

We start with the setting — a typical Episcopal church — and those moments before the service begins.

Chapter Three

Discovering What God Is Like:
The Word

The service we are about to explore is divided into two halves. The first half is called the "Word," and the second is called "Holy Communion." In this chapter we explore the first half. The focus in the first half is to explain to us the nature of the God we are worshiping and to enter into God's presence through Scripture, confession, and worship. This half of the service is loosely based on what we would find in a Jewish synagogue service. The synagogue has a mixture of Scripture readings, the singing of a psalm, prayers, and a sermon; this half of the service takes the Christian Scriptures and weaves them together with music, prayer, and reflection. At every stage, we shall find that there is embedded in the liturgical moment a life principle — a way of looking at life made possible by the liturgy.

THE MOMENTS BEFORE A SERVICE BEGINS

The first thing to notice as you step into a church is the setting. Episcopal churches work hard on the setting. Episcopal churches are places of beauty — stained glass, carved woodwork, flowers, and altar hangings. As we enter the church, we are invited to surround ourselves with the beauty of creation and the story of Christ, with a sense of the saints and the distinctive history of the particular place we are in. We should feast on this reality, appreciating it as one does fine art. The setting introduces the main themes of the service that follows. As we look at the cross at the front of the church and the images of Christ in the windows, so we are invited to recognize that Christ was human. The Creator of all that is relates to us. And the images of the saints in the windows are there to remind us of all the others, who have already been transformed by God. As we sit in church looking at the saints, it is good to remember that all the problems in our lives God has dealt with in other human lives. And some of those problem lives are now saints who adorn the windows we are looking at. There is hope for all of us in the saints.

As we find our seats, it is helpful to prepare ourselves for the occasion in which we will participate. We have to be open to what God wants to do. So we pause and collect our thoughts, and as the people gather we offer our lives in all their complexity to God.

THE ARRIVAL

Liturgical Life Principle 1: The faith of the cross invites us to live while acknowledging the reality of suffering and death.

In preparation for the service we have already noticed the cross at the front of the church. Now as the service starts, we stand as the crucifer (the person carrying the cross) leads the procession.

In the Episcopal tradition, one stands as a mark of respect. So we stand or kneel to pray, and sit to listen to readings and the sermon. In the same way we would stand in the presence of an important dignitary, so we stand to enter the presence of God. We also stand as the choir and clergy process in, led by the crucifer carrying the cross.

The cross is rich in symbolism. If you think about it, there is something rather odd about the cross being the central Christian symbol. If Jesus had lived and died today, the symbol would have been an electric chair. The cross is shocking. It is a symbol of judicial execution by power (that is, the State).

As we prepare ourselves for the work that God wants to do in our lives to allow us to live in healthy and authentic ways, the cross is a vitally important place to start. The cross reminds us that Christianity does not equate healthy living with a pain-free, suffering-free existence. Death is a reality that is confronted constantly — indeed, at the heart of this service. Death is a challenge; we need to live life in the light of death. This day, this week, this year might be our last. Finding a constructive way to live with that possibility is a vitally important part of healthy living. God's encounter with death is put symbolically at the front of the procession and the church. Christians believe that God in Christ created the miracle of "redemption" out of that encounter. Christians believe that the "sting of death" was eliminated by that encounter. Christians believe that out of the despair of Good Friday the promise of resurrection Sunday was created. As the cross passes, some will bow, thereby acknowledging that healthy living needs to come to terms with mortality, not in a negative way, in ways that recognize the miracle of the transformation of death made possible by Jesus.

Authentic living means that we acknowledge the reality of suffering and death. There is no evasion in this setting. As we engage with the liturgy, we will find that there is no explanation or excuse provided for suffering. But it is constantly and steadfastly recognized. Suffering and death are a dreadful reality. Right at the outset, we are not allowed to hide. We are going to recognize that reality and invite that reality to make a difference.

When we face the reality of death, it clarifies what really matters. Never separate from those you love without making sure that they know you love them. It is so important not to let the trivial get in the way of the important. As we look at the cross at the front of the church and bow as the processional cross passes, these are the thoughts we are invited to entertain. The work of making us healthy and authentic has begun.

+ **For meditation:** Christianity is a faith that recognizes the reality of death. Reflect on your attitude toward death. Invite God into your fears and anxiety. Reflect on your values in the life of death.

COLLECT FOR PURITY

Liturgical Life Principle 2: God wants to do the work; God wants us to let him.

> Almighty God, to you all hearts are open, all desires known, and from you no secrets are hid: Cleanse the thoughts of our hearts by the inspiration of your Holy Spirit, that we may perfectly love you, and worthily magnify your holy Name; through Christ our Lord. *Amen.* [BCP p. 355]

◆ ◆ ◆

Much of the service is spent in prayer. Healthy and authentic living depends on prayer. Here we have a collect (which should be pronounced call-ect), which simply means a prayer that "collects together" certain issues for the congregation. A major theme of this service is that God has provided the resources for living a transformed life and we need simply to reach out and seize these resources. The opening prayer prepares us for the work that God will do during this hour in God's presence. It is called the collect for purity. It is a prayer for preparation, a prayer that God will make us pure as we embark on the challenge of worship.

> **The collect for purity** should remind us of Psalm 51. Originally it was a prayer to be said by the priest as "he" (as it was for centuries) prepared for the service. In the 1552 rite, it was included as a prayer that all should identify with. Archbishop Thomas Cranmer (1489–1556) made it the opening prayer of the service.

The stress of being human means that most of us enter the worship space preoccupied and distracted. The liturgy recognizes that we come into the service with a host of entirely legitimate worries and concerns. Our work might be difficult and stressful, a relationship might not be going well, we might be in physical pain, or we might be in a state of high anxiety over the growing pains of our son or daughter. God knows exactly what we are thinking: our hearts and desires are all known to God. In this collect we invite God to grant us the gift of focus. God needs a quiet mind focused on the miracle of grace to facilitate and realize that miracle. We ask God to calm us and focus us.

In so doing, we can see an important principle at work. God wants us to live healthy and authentic lives. There is a beautiful simplicity in all this. The Creator of everything that is needs some space in our lives to transform our lives. A large part of the liturgical transformation is simply letting God do what God wants to do.

♦ **For meditation:** Lift up each anxiety. Name the anxiety. Then offer that anxiety to God.

GLORIA: SONG OF PRAISE

Liturgical Life Principle 3: In worship we recognize what matters, and we start to sort out what matters in our life.

When appointed, the following hymn or some other song of praise is sung or said, all standing:

> Glory to God in the highest,
>   and peace to his people on earth.
>
> Lord God, heavenly King,
> almighty God and Father,
>   we worship you, we give you thanks,
>   we praise you for your glory.
> Lord Jesus Christ, only Son of the Father,
> Lord God, Lamb of God,
> you take away the sin of the world:
>   have mercy on us;
> you are seated at the right hand of the Father:
>   receive our prayer.
>
> For you alone are the Holy One,
> you alone are the Lord,
> you alone are the Most High,
>   Jesus Christ,
>   with the Holy Spirit,
>   in the glory of God the Father. Amen.
>
> [BCP p. 356]

◆ ◆ ◆

The work of preparation over, we now move into a song of praise. Normally this is the Gloria, but sometimes it is the Trisagion or the Kyrie Eleison. Worship is like breathing: it is absolutely essential for our survival. When we worship, we connect with that which enables us to be. The Creator sustains everything. We cannot exist without God enabling us to exist. When we worship, we acknowledge that reality, and, as a result, we see everything differently.

The greatest sin of all is to imagine we are self-sufficient. It is, of course, an absurd sin. We depend on a million things for existence at any one moment — air, water, food, space, time. The act of worshiping God is an act of recognition — recognition of our dependence on all these aspects of creation provided by God. But more, it is also a recognition that our very gift of consciousness is enabled by the grace of God. No one is entitled to be born; life is a gift. So worship is the creature acknowledging a God-enabled reality that we receive.

THE KYRIE
(LORD HAVE MERCY)
[BCP p. 356]

In the original context the term "Lord" would have been applied to the Roman emperor. This is a very ancient prayer of acclamation, introduced into Christian liturgy in the fourth century.

THE TRISAGION
[BCP p. 356]

Holy God,
Holy and Mighty,
Holy Immortal One,
Have mercy upon us.

This is a hymn imported from the Greek Orthodox liturgy. It was very popular with Martin Luther. Sometimes it is repeated three times.

THE GLORIA IN EXCELSIS DEO
(GLORY TO GOD IN THE HIGHEST)
The Song of Praise
[BCP p. 356]

Since the fourth century, the Gloria has been used in the morning office. In certain very ancient rites, it was confined to special festive days, but by the twelfth century it was often used on Sundays. To be consistent with the different moods of the church year, it should not be sung during Lent or Advent.

When we worship, it is important that we don't mix God up with a very big person. God is "personal," but not a person. God has characteristics that we link with human agency; for example, God loves, decides, forgives, and judges. And given that these are actions we link with persons (vegetables, for example, don't perform actions), we talk of God as personal. But God does not have a physical body. Indeed the doctrine of creation — that God underpins and enables everything to be — makes the idea of God having a physical body absurd. A physical body cannot be everywhere. God is spirit — holding everything within God's life. (Christians do, however, believe in the Incarnation — namely, that God became human; God as Creator God does not have a body.)

Although God shares a certain similarity with "consciousness" (because consciousness enables agency), God is not an ego. This is important because it is easy to end up rather bemused by worship. It sometimes looks as if we are telling this giant ego in the sky how big and great "he" is. Indeed the way some Christians talk, it sounds like God set up the universe to require worship from all God's creatures and threatens to condemn to eternal punishment anyone who refuses. This makes God sound pathetic, like God is such an insecure ego that God needs lots of reassurance. This is open to the telling criticism of the Welsh philosopher Rush Rhees: "If my first and chief reason for worshipping God had to be a belief that a super-Frankenstein would blast me to hell if I did not, then I hope I should have the decency to tell this being, who is named Almighty God, to go ahead and blast."[5] If worship is telling this rather insecure ego in the sky how great he is, then it does sound, at the very least, silly, if not downright immoral.

Worship is not telling a giant ego in the sky how jolly big God is. In worshiping, we bow the knee and recognize the qualities of absolute worth in our Creator God. We recognize in God those qualities of supreme bliss, supreme love, supreme order, and supreme beauty.

Worship is both our recognizing our dependence on the Creator and the recognition of what ultimately matters. When we worship God, we recognize that the values of love, beauty, and justice have ultimate value. These matter most. Worship is incompatible with a life of hatred, ugliness, and injustice. This point is made forcefully by the prophet Amos:

> I hate, I despise your festivals,
> and I take no delight in your solemn assemblies.
> Even though you offer me your burnt-offerings and grain-
> offerings,
> I will not accept them;
> and the offerings of well-being of your fatted animals
> I will not look upon.

Take away from me the noise of your songs;
   I will not listen to the melody of your harps.
But let justice roll down like waters,
   and righteousness like an ever-flowing stream.
                  (Amos 5:21–24)

The point Amos is making is that we cannot live oppressing our neighbor and, at the same time, worship God. One cannot affirm injustice six days a week and affirm that justice is of ultimate worth on Sunday. When we worship, we start to sort out what ultimately matters.

At the Gloria all sorts of hard work of healthy living is starting to happen. We are locating ourselves. We are recognizing the gift of being: the fact that it is a privilege that God loves us and enables us to be. Every day is a gift. We are also sorting out our value hierarchy. How do I know that certain activities are good and others are bad? How do I know that some things matter more than other things? In worship we have the answers. In worship we recognize the good. In worship we sort out what ultimately matters.

Healthy and authentic living requires healthy priorities. So, for example, in my life there are three activities that are important: video games (which I really enjoy playing), being a dean of a seminary (my work), and spending time with my wife and son (my duty and joy as a husband and father). In the act of worship, we should start to see what matters most and what matters less. The video games are fun, but less important than being the dean of a seminary, which brings certain responsibilities. My work is important, but it is less important than my relationships, especially with those whom God has placed closest to me. As I worship, I acknowledge what really matters. As I see what really matters, I can see what matters less. In saying the Gloria, I should allow myself to be challenged. In acknowledging that Jesus is the Most High, I examine my life and explore whether Jesus really is the most high in my life. As I stand in the presence of undistorted, ultimately good values, I ask the question, "Are my values distorted?" Am I spending too much time playing golf and thereby neglecting other priorities? Am I spending too much time at work and thereby neglecting my relationship with my wife and son?

Worship is a challenge. This process of reflection will not happen as a result of simply saying the Gloria once. Fortunately, there are several opportunities to acknowledge the nature of God in this service. We need constantly to return and stand respectfully before God and acknowledge who God is. In so doing, we find ourselves challenged to live differently.

♦ **For meditation:** In the light of the nature of God, reflect on your values. Have you got your value hierarchy appropriately ordered?

THE GREETING

Liturgical Life Principle 4: In the Christian Liturgical Greeting, we invoke the Creator of everything that is to be part of each other's endeavors.

The Celebrant says to the people

> The Lord be with you.

People And also with you.

Celebrant Let us pray. [BCP p. 357]

♦ ♦ ♦

Just watching the crucifer with the cross should have challenged us to think differently. However, the greeting is just astonishing. A sure way of getting the attention of a group of Episcopalians is for someone to say, "The Lord be with you." And with a reflex reaction, the reply comes, "And also with you."

A greeting reflects value. In different cultures the greeting takes different forms. Muslims, for example, greet each other with *As-Salâmu Alaykum,* which is Arabic for "peace be upon you." The exchange creates a framework for the encounter that commits the parties to a framework of peace. The Christian liturgical greeting is different. We ask that God Almighty, Creator of everything that is, should be with you. Consider for a moment how big God is. God is the Creator of this planet, this solar system (with the sun 93 million miles away), this Milky Way galaxy (which is over 100,000 light years across), and millions of other galaxies. And we are greeting one another with a request that the Creator of everything that is should be with you.

This sense of "being with" is not simply a recognition of the reality of creation. It is not simply that God made us and is everywhere

> **The Greeting** is normally called the "salutation."
> It is a biblical greeting found in the book of Ruth
> where Boaz greets those working in the field with the
> phrase "The Lord be with you" (Ruth 2:4). It has been
> an important part of Christian liturgy for centuries.

that makes this true. We are also asking that the power, love, and peace of God might be with you. Again this is a recurring theme of this book (as we shall discover when we come to the blessing). We start and finish the service with a reminder that the Divine should be present — present as a resource, present as an enabler, and present to facilitate healthy and authentic living.

+ **For meditation:** Marvel on the claim that the Creator of the universe is deeply interested in you.

COLLECT FOR THE DAY

Liturgical Life Principle 5: We focus on different aspects of the healthy and authentic living project at different times of the church year.

This opening collect links moments in the church year with the readings and sermon that follow in the rest of the service. At this point, we have another background tool coming into play: the church year. The church year makes time sacred: it turns the passing of time into a way of reflecting about our relationship with God. The church year moves from season to season, not in a linear way but more like a spiral. Each ending is a new beginning. We start in Advent, the four weeks prior to Christmas. This is a period of preparation: we are reminded of the movement of time and our obligation to constantly prepare to receive the grace that God wants to give us. The past is a given (in the case of Advent, a past made up of the stories of countless Jewish men and women who were faithful and used by God to create the Christ child possibility), and the present becomes a possibility for divine grace and providence.

Christmas is the season of celebration. We ponder the miracle of the Divine becoming a human infant. It discloses to us a truth about a God who understands vulnerability, fear, and dependence. We are able to pray to God confident that God understands us. The healthy and authentic living project is made possible by a God who knows precisely what the demands of human living involve from the inside.

In early January we embark on the season of Epiphany. The encounter with Christ is not simply for Christians; it also touches the life of the entire world. Astrologers from the East come and worship the Christ child. We are reminded of our interconnection with all humanity — the call of God is to all people. In the act of giving gifts we are challenged to reflect on our gifts and our obligation to give back to God.

Lent is soon upon us. The healthy and authentic living project often involves struggle. And our own worst enemy is ourselves. There are inside each and every one of us destructive propensities desperate to come out. For some of us, it is the tendency to spend too much money: to make yet another charge to the credit card. We know this is unwise, but for some mysterious reason we still do it. For others, it is constantly fussing about clothes and always wanting a new outfit. Deep down, we know this new outfit isn't necessary, but we buy it anyway. More seriously, it is the successful businessperson who doesn't need to pad the expense account, but does so anyway, and then watches a successful career disintegrate. Or it is the happily married husband or wife who can't resist the business trip fling and then watches a marriage disintegrate amid pain and anguish. We need to work against these destructive propensities. And Lent is the period of confession, repentance, and examination. So as we move through each season in the church year, we focus on a different aspect of the healthy and authentic living project.

Easter is where the drama of death and despair meet resurrection and hope. It is the heart of the Christian drama. It is the moment of our redemption, when the miracle of God's action transforms our situation. Pentecost is the moment when the agency of God in our present is celebrated. We are constantly reminded at this moment that the past events of creation and incarnation are available to us in the present through the Holy Spirit. Pentecost eases into "ordinary time" when we do the hard work of discipleship day by day. The symbolism of the church year is captured in this opening collect.

THE CHRISTIAN CALENDAR

Advent (four weeks prior to Christmas)	A period of preparation for the coming of Christ.
Christmas Day (twelve days; the season lasts for one or two Sundays)	The birthday of Jesus: the birth of the Incarnation of God.
Epiphany, January 6 (the season lasts for six weeks)	The visit of the Magi from the East to pay homage to the baby Jesus; the season during which we experience the light of Christ in the world.
Ash Wednesday (the start of Lent)	A day for remembering our mortality and starting the period of Lent.
Lent (a total of forty days, excluding Sundays, before Easter)	We recall the forty days that Jesus spent in the wilderness.
Palm Sunday (the sixth Sunday in Lent and the start of Holy Week)	Recalling the day that Jesus entered into Jerusalem in triumph.
Holy Week	Recalling the events that culminated in the death of Jesus.
Easter (the season lasts five weeks)	During the season of Easter we focus on the resurrection appearances of the Risen Christ.
Ascension Day (the fortieth day after Easter)	The day Jesus ascended into heaven.
Pentecost (the fiftieth day after Easter)	The day the Holy Spirit descended on the disciples; the birthday of the church.
Trinity Sunday (the Sunday after Pentecost)	A celebration of the church's affirmation of the doctrine of the Trinity.
Season of Pentecost (normally about twenty-five weeks)	Green and growing time.

◆ **For meditation:** Notice how the church year makes time holy. Reflect on the passing of time and how important it is to live into the cycle of the church year.

LESSONS AND SERMON

Liturgical Life Principle 6: The nature of the God seeking to transform us is the one revealed in the Eternal Word, conveyed to us in the Written Word, and made present to us in the Proclaimed Word.

Others can help us with the healthy and authentic living project. After all, this is a divine project for all humanity, and it has been going on for centuries. So the readings from the Bible, two or three, and a psalm connect us with the broader narrative of which we are a small part. In addition, these readings disclose to us what God is like and how God relates to our lives. They are the Word of God. It is here that we learn of the Eternal Word made present in Christ, which is captured in the Written Word (of Scripture), and then the tricky task of the preacher is to deliver the Proclaimed Word (making the Word present to us now) in the sermon.

The first reading comes from the Old Testament, which of course is the Hebrew Scriptures originating with the Jewish people. The divine project is deeply rooted in the drama of the Jewish people. We are all children of Abraham; he birthed the traditions of Judaism, Christianity, and Islam. As we have already noted at the start of this chapter, this part of the service is structurally grounded in the Jewish synagogue service: the mix of readings from the Scriptures, preaching, a psalm, and prayers are all the basic ingredients of a synagogue service. As the Old Testament lesson is read, we consider God's action and disclosure among the Jewish people.

Sometimes the Old Testament reading is replaced with a reading from the book of Acts. This is the story of the emergence of the early church. It recounts the drama of the struggles of the early Christians as they witnessed to the risen Lord. It is a spectacular narrative, which includes almost everything — persecution, imprisonment, miracles, arguments, as well as rousing preaching and a large number of converts.

The second reading comes from an epistle. An epistle is a letter, and most of the epistles of the New Testament were written by that dynamic Apostle of the first century, St. Paul. Paul had the difficult task of interpreting the word of God in Jesus for the early church. Christians very wisely collected his writings to include in the canon of the New Testament. (They also added a few letters that they thought were written by Paul but were not.)

In between the two readings we have the psalm. The psalms comprise the oldest hymn book in the Abrahamic traditions, a book found in our Old Testament. In any human life, the healthy and authentic living project is sometimes a joy, sometimes difficult, and sometimes almost unbearable. Often it is events beyond our control that make life close to impossible. The parent who loses a child or the employee who is suddenly laid off experiences fear, anger, and perhaps excruciating pain. The psalms affirm all these responses. Psalm 142, for example, is a classic psalm of lament:

> With my voice I cry to the Lord;
>   with my voice I make supplication to the Lord.
> I pour out my complaint before him;
>   I tell my trouble before him. (Ps. 142:1–2)

This psalm highlights moments of anger, loneliness, and pain. Pulsating through these psalms are the moods of living. For every human struggle, there is an appropriate psalm.

Healthy and authentic living is not a denial of how we feel. We are not promised that we will never be unhappy. Pain, suffering, and death come to all of us and often tragically. We are allowed to be angry with God. Indeed both health and authenticity require that sometimes we are angry. To deny these feelings would be inauthentic and potentially very unhealthy. At times we should be angry with God. This we know because of the witness of the psalms.

Next we come to the reading of the Gospel. The four Gospels — Matthew, Mark, Luke, and John — form the first part of the New Testament. They tell us the story of Jesus. These are ancient biographies that invite us to imitate the words and deeds of Jesus. Christians believe that in Jesus we have the Eternal Word disclosed to us. So we stand and face the deacon or the priest who is reading the Gospel. The good news — the literal meaning of the word "Gospel" — comes to us (symbolized by the Gospel often being read in the midst of the congregation). Healthy and authentic living depends on this: we need to receive the good news. We need to receive the divine action promised in Christ. God has done the work here; the response of trust and cooperation is all that is needed.

The preaching of the Word follows the Gospel. Preaching has an important place in the Episcopal Church, but it is only one of many tools involved in the project of healthy and authentic living. Preaching is not the primary focus of the service as it is in some Christian traditions. It runs parallel with and is preparation for Holy Communion. A good sermon connects the readings to our situation and our lives. It should bring hope and challenge. It should prepare us for the second part of the service, which we will look at in the next chapter, namely, Holy Communion.

♦ **For meditation:** The Bible is, in many ways, a shocking book. Every human reality is found in these pages. Meditate on the God who encounters us in the confusion and problems of being human.

THE NICENE CREED

Liturgical Life Principle 7: We trust the God revealed in Jesus of Nazareth to transform us.

We believe in one God,
the Father, the Almighty,
maker of heaven and earth,
of all that is, seen and unseen.

We believe in one Lord, Jesus Christ,
the only Son of God,
eternally begotten of the Father,
God from God, Light from Light,
true God from true God,
begotten, not made,
of one Being with the Father.
Through him all things were made.
For us and for our salvation
he came down from heaven:
by the power of the Holy Spirit
he became incarnate from the Virgin Mary,
and was made man.
For our sake he was crucified under Pontius Pilate;
he suffered death and was buried.

On the third day he rose again
    in accordance with the Scriptures;
he ascended into heaven
    and is seated at the right hand of the Father.
He will come again in glory to judge the living and the dead,
    and his kingdom will have no end.

We believe in the Holy Spirit, the Lord, the giver of life,
    who proceeds from the Father and the Son.
With the Father and the Son he is worshiped and glorified.
He has spoken through the Prophets.
We believe in one holy catholic and apostolic Church.
We acknowledge one baptism for the forgiveness of sins.
We look for the resurrection of the dead,
    and the life of the world to come. Amen.

[BCP pp. 358–59]

◆ ◆ ◆

After a moment's silence, when we reflect on the God who has been disclosed to us in the encounter with the Word, we all stand, face the altar, and respond by affirming our faith. It is our response to what we have heard. We take ownership of the cosmic narrative about God's disclosure to humanity and make it our own. The Creed begins by affirming the source of everything that is and then moves on to tell the story of Jesus becoming human. It concludes with an affirmation of the work of the Holy Spirit in the church, one baptism, and our hope for life to come.

There are many teachings that are not in the Creed. There is no explicit theory explaining how Jesus saves us; there is no theory of biblical inspiration. It is important to distinguish between first-order issues and second-order issues. A first-order issue speaks to the fundamental identity of the Christian drama; a second-order issue is one which is less important and about which Christians can and will disagree. It is important for us to struggle with the ideas in the Creed. We can, however, be more relaxed about items not in the Creed. "Struggling" means that we remain in conversation with the Creed. It is often said that the opposite of faith is not doubt but certainty, and there is some truth in this. The Christian obligation is to seek to understand and trust the Christian claim that God was in Christ. The exact way we understand that claim has changed in the history of Christian doctrine and will change for us as we think

> **The Nicene Creed** was so called because it emerged at the Council of Nicaea in 325 C.E. More strictly it should be called the Nicene-Constantinopolitan Creed because it was completed at the Council of Constantinople in 381 C.E. At the Third Council of Toledo in Spain (589 C.E.), the Creed was introduced into the service. Slowly the practice was incorporated throughout the church.

about our beliefs. This is fine. To be a Christian, however, we are obligated to be in the conversation.

The Creed starts with the work of the Father. When we talk of God the Father, we are talking about the aspect of God that enables everything to be. God is the Creator. God is not simply the origin of everything, the entity that started the universe. God is also the one who enables everything to continue to be from moment to moment. In this sense God underpins absolutely everything.

The Creed moves on to tell the story of the Son becoming human, dying, and then rising from death. This narrative captures the central claim of Christianity. For Christians, the definitive disclosure of God is a life. We are constantly reading and interpreting a life. The Creed explains how the Eternal Word completely interpenetrates Jesus of Nazareth, thereby enabling us to read from his life truths about God and God's relationship to humanity. His life is revelatory of God.

Some Christians struggle with all this doctrine, and of course God understands that we are all in different places. It is, however, necessary for us to know what God is like (or at least to have some idea of what God is like). Otherwise we will end up being "agnostics"; we will just guess what God is like. All knowledge of God depends on God telling us.

For Christians, the Word of God is disclosed in the life, death, and resurrection of Jesus, which in turn is conveyed to us in the written words of Scripture. Our primary access to the past is a text; in the readings we receive the Word of God (which is Christ).

In the final section of the Creed, the focus is on the work of the Holy Spirit. It is the Holy Spirit who enables God to be present to us today. According to the book of Acts, the Spirit came on the day of Pentecost to equip the church with the power to bring the good news of God's saving acts to humanity. With the affirmation of the Holy Spirit, we move quickly to affirm the reality of the church and the centrality of baptism (the sacrament that marks initiation into the church). As we say these words, we are invited to reflect on the graciousness of God, who provides for us a community that can help us with our healthy and authentic living project.

+ **For meditation:** Reflect on your understanding of these key beliefs of the Creed. For those aspects of the creed you find a challenge, read a book (see the list of books at the end of this volume) that might help you understand the doctrine.

PRAYER

Liturgical Life Principle 8: We give God our worries. And by bringing the worries of the world to God, we begin to locate our own worries.

For many people, simply coping is a remarkable achievement. We just want to survive: we don't want our house repossessed; we want to keep our job; we want our children to be healthy and safe. The joy of this moment in our liturgy is that the challenge of coping will now be met in the presence of the God who made us and loves us. And so we stand (again out of respect) in the presence of the Almighty and offer our requests.[6]

One important part of the healthy and authentic living project is to be sure that we pray for others. Praying for the world, praying for the president and the Congress are tasks that most people undertake only corporately. When we are alone with God, our prayers are much more personal. But in the healthy and authentic living project, we are obliged to locate our worries about ourselves in the wider context of the entire world. This is a very precious moment.

For the truth about living in modern America is that however stressed we are about our lives, others in the world are coping with much more stress. So as we pause and remember leaders of our country and the world and the suffering of the people in, for example, Iraq, we are invited to remember that our problems are significant but others have problems much more significant.

Prayer, however, is more than just locating our problem. We are asking God to enter the situation and solve the problem. At this point prayer seems puzzling. Are we informing God about things that God doesn't already know about? Are we persuading God to do things that God wouldn't otherwise do? How does God work?

The practice of public prayer has its roots in Judaism, which has a strong emphasis on prayer in both public worship and in home worship. For Christianity, the practice of prayer in public worship goes back to the second century. The structure of biddings with a response is seen as early as the fourth century.

Many Christians have problems with prayer for two reasons. The first is that they see God as some immutable entity that already knows in complete detail how the future is going to pan out. The second is that they see the universe as a big machine, where each segment is determined by a prior segment. We need, however, to see both God and the world differently. A more biblical picture of God recognizes that God embarked on this project of creation by creating humans who have genuine freedom. God wanted a universe where love can flourish, and love requires people who are genuinely free. Freedom requires a universe that is stable, predictable, and yet open to human decision and agency. If I am going to be responsible for "hitting" someone, there needs to be a stable universe where I understand the connection between my decision to strike and the subsequent action of someone being hurt. This also means that it is impossible for anyone to know with any certainty how free people are going to behave. Even God cannot know the logically impossible. So God is constantly facing many possible futures for this world.

As a result God is constantly working to create more loving opportunities to be realized in this world, and because love cannot be compelled, God cannot simply override the structures of creation and force love on the world. God requires our free cooperation in terms of both action and prayer.

One joy of living in the twenty-first century is that we have some sense of how God works; our picture of the universe has changed. God is working within the contours of the world that God has made. The image of the world as a big machine made prayer difficult. We ended up with a capricious God who is constantly interfering with the machine. But with the new physics the machine image is gone. Our picture is much more holistic. Human beings, for example, are much more than the sum of our parts. And the picture is open and radically indeterminate: many odd things happen at the sub-atomic level.

Now we can see a little more clearly how God has set things up. Naturally God has the power to create an entirely different universe, but in the one that God chose to create, God has determined that the cooperation of humanity is important to God. God needs us — out of love for God and for each other — to behave in ways that further love and to pray constantly for love to triumph. Prayer opens up space in the universe for God to act. Keith Ward puts it well when he writes:

> Sin closes off possibilities of Divine action; whereas obedient love opens up new channels for Divine action. When we show such love by praying for others, we may open up channels of healing that God can use; creatures and creator can cooperate in making the world more transparent to Divine influence.[7]

There are two related aspects of prayer that God uses. The first is this opening up of the universe. If a butterfly flapping its wings in Chicago can cause a hurricane in China, then a person praying can create the space for God to heal another person. The butterfly flapping its wings is an allusion to the famous discovery of quantum physics that very small fluctuations at the quantum level can have dramatic effects elsewhere in the cosmos because of the inter-connectedness of the cosmos. It isn't that God is restricted to the mysterious quantum universe, but that the intrinsic interconnected-ness and openness of the universe has made human and divine agency possible. The act of healing is a divine action that uses the space created by prayer in creation to work with the mechanism that God has built into creation to heal. To simply "heal" everyone all the time would involve constantly overriding the structures of creation and would erode human freedom. But as Scripture prom-ises us: God hears our prayers and responds to our prayers. God takes all our prayers into account as they arise. And God works with the space that they create within creation for divine action.

This takes us to the second aspect of prayer that God uses. When we pray our egotistical and destructive tendencies are challenged. One major problem for God is that countless creatures are exercising their freedom to opt for evil, hatred, and selfishness. Christians call this "sin." When we are spending our time, however, opening ourselves to God, we are not using that time to be cruel, selfish, unkind, or inconsiderate. Indeed, the very act of being in the presence of God makes us less likely to be cruel and selfish.

The net result is that our prayers are an energy that God uses to perform miracles in human lives. In much the same way as the causal connection between the butterfly's wings and the hurricane is impossible to establish, so the connection between God's agency and the various healing factors on, say, a person's leg are impossible to establish. But we can now see how these connections are possible. So we pray in confidence that God is hearing our prayers and using the space we create to further the demands of love.

◆ **For meditation:** Reflect on the percentage of your time you spend praying about immediate and personal matters compared with the time you spend praying for the world and international affairs. Spend some time trying to create a better balance.

CONFESSION OF SIN

Liturgical Life Principle 9: Transformation doesn't happen overnight. There will be struggles and areas that we must continue to let God work on.

The Deacon or Celebrant says

Let us confess our sins against God and our neighbor.

Silence may be kept.

Minister and People

Most merciful God,
we confess that we have sinned against you
in thought, word, and deed,
by what we have done,

and by what we have left undone.
We have not loved you with our whole heart;
we have not loved our neighbors as ourselves.
We are truly sorry and we humbly repent.
For the sake of your Son Jesus Christ,
have mercy on us and forgive us;
that we may delight in your will,
and walk in your ways,
to the glory of your Name. Amen.

The Bishop when present, or the Priest, stands and says

Almighty God have mercy on you, forgive you all your sins
through our Lord Jesus Christ, strengthen you in all goodness,
and by the power of the Holy Spirit keep you in eternal life.
Amen.   [BCP p. 360]

◆ ◆ ◆

Prayer includes confession. Even though we all want to be good (at
least on our better and more clear-sighted days), we all find it difficult. The healthy and authentic living project takes very seriously
that there is much inside us that makes healthy and authentic living
difficult.

It is odd how we insist on making difficult situations worse. We
are in an argument with a friend and know that bringing a particular topic up will only make the situation worse, but we do so
anyway. Or we know that this bit of gossip is damaging, but we
cannot resist passing it on — in confidence! Or we entertain a de-
licious fantasy that is not constructive and is really encouraging a
temptation, but we cannot resist replaying the fantasy in our mind.
Or we are endlessly preoccupied with things, even though there is
less and less space to put them in our home, but our "need" to have
these things just gets the better of us — and we simply must have
that new outfit or new pair of shoes. Or we know that by staying
late at the office we are putting a considerable strain on our marriage and our relationship with our children, but our addiction to
work means we have no intention of ordering our life differently.
Or we are unable to be calm in the car and so easily flash our head-
lights and hit the horn, adding to our own stress levels and those
of others, but strangely we just enjoy doing it. And so the list goes

on. We are constantly behaving in ways that make us — in the long run — unhappy.

The Episcopal liturgy is intensely realistic. You will always have something to confess, so every week you have the opportunity to do so. In fact an interesting side of people really advanced along the healthy and authentic living project is that their goodness makes them aware of how bad they are, so the "saints" among us tend to confess even more than regular people. Regular people have so many major things to work on that we haven't the time to reach into the murky places of motive and underlying disposition. Yet genuine confession must involve the intent to work seriously on our destructive tendencies. If taken seriously, the frequent practice of confession will slowly bring about a change in our lives. We will become better, healthier persons.

> **Public confession** of sin arose during the Reformation. A popular place for the confession of sin was during the Great Thanksgiving prayer; in the current prayer book, the confession of sin is part of the preparation for the Sacrament.

At this point in the service we stand or kneel before God. The confession is comprehensive. It includes our interior life (the imaginative life of the mind), our discourse (our conversation, our propensity to gossip), and our actions (everything we do). It includes both acts and omissions. Often it is the things we do not do, for example, visit a relative in the hospital, that expose our selfishness. Then we have the two great commandments. Are we really focused on the good, the beautiful, and the true (which is really what loving God with our whole heart involves)? And are we really loving our neighbors as ourselves?

Loving your neighbor as yourself means that the lack of "self-love" is a sin. Loving others does not mean that we become doormats. It does not mean that we are so selfless that the self is no longer present. To love others we must have a self to love with, and we are obligated to confess any failure of "self-care."

Finally we say that we are "sorry" and that we "humbly repent." What follows is the fresh slate: the priest is the channel of God's grace — one that ensures that we know about God's forgiveness of us, one that communicates to us our forgiven status within the life and death of Jesus of Nazareth.

At the end of the confession, we know that God wants another week to work on our weaknesses. So we stand with the intention to live an improved life. We also know that we are going to be back here next week. So we don't beat ourselves up in a destructive way when we slip again. But neither do we resign ourselves to the slips. We are going to step forward and work on our destructive habits. We are going to be better parents, employees, spouses, and friends.

The fact that this is a public confession of sin, which occurs in community, highlights another aspect of the moment, namely, this is when the community faces up to "corporate and institutional sin." As a white, male Englishman, I am very conscious that I am enjoying the privilege made possible by my white male English predecessors, who exploited and oppressed to secure resources for subsequent generations. As we make this public confession of sin, we should acknowledge how we indirectly benefit from the sins of others. Certain brands of cheap coffee are available to us because of the exploitation of a workforce in the two-thirds world; men occupy more positions of power because they have denied those positions to women; white exploitation of the nonwhite has left a trail of destruction around the globe.

Confession always entails a commitment to be different. We should use this moment to recognize our obligation to challenge injustice and do what we can to make the world a different place.

+ **For meditation:** Identify one particular area you are constantly revisiting in confession. Ask God to provide the resources to transform that area.

THE PEACE

Liturgical Life Principle 10: Rather than harboring anger and resentment toward others (both past and present), we need to let the peace of the Lord bring a calm that enables growth.

All stand. The Celebrant says to the people

> The peace of the Lord be always with you.

People   And also with you.

Then the Ministers and People may greet one another in the name of the Lord. [BCP p. 360]

◆ ◆ ◆

Made right with God, we now need to make sure we are right with everyone else. So we are invited to exchange the peace. At this moment when we move from the Word part of the service to the Holy Communion part of the service, we remind ourselves of the admonition of Jesus, that before coming into the Father's presence, we should be sure that we are at peace with our neighbor (Matt. 5:23–24).

The peace operates on a number of levels. On a very important but basic level, it is an opportunity to share the peace with someone who is different from us and whom we might ignore in another place. We reach out and recognize our obligation to be at peace across difference (difference of style, ethnicity, race, gender, class).

On another level, it is a recognition that we must avoid the stress that is linked with our inability to get along with others. From the angry exchange with someone we love to the deep, abiding unforgiven resentment against someone in our past, we often live life "not at peace" with our neighbor.

In an ideal universe, the peace would be used as an opportunity to reach out to a person who has hurt us during the week. Perhaps we should be invited at that moment to use our cell phones to call the person who upset us at the office. At the very least, in the act of reaching out to the people around us, we do — in our hearts — reach out to those who have made us angry and distressed.

There is enormous power in coming to "peace" with each other. Anger and resentment are destructive energies that consume and destroy the moment. We spend so much time being mad at someone that we fail to enjoy the many things that are good about our lives.

The need for peace extends to the past. Many of us live with an anger directed to people in their past — for example, the woman still angry with her husband, who left her ten years ago, or the man still angry because his father neglected him as a child.

Our reaching out and exchanging the peace symbolizes our reaching out beyond the church, both to the present (the people we are finding it difficult to work with) and to the past (the people who hurt us months or even years ago). It is the moment in the service when we declare that we are going to bring "the peace of the Lord" to our relationships. We are going to surrender the pain, misery, and anger and invite God to bring a calmness and peace to our lives.

Living in a state of simmering rage is unhelpful, futile, and an additional punishment of ourselves. Surrendering the anger and coming to a state of divine peace turns the present moment into a constructive, energetic, liberating state of genuine freedom.

So we arrive at the end of the first part of the service. God has already challenged us and made us look at the world differently. We are already far advanced along the path of the healthy and authentic living project.

- **For meditation:** Reflect on those in your past who hurt you. Offer those lives up to God and ask for the peace of the Lord to make the difference, thereby enabling you to put the hurt behind you.

Chapter Four

Approaching the Eucharist

We are now ready to move into the second part of the service. Here the focus is on Holy Communion. Having listened to the Word, affirmed our faith, confessed our sins, and given of ourselves to others, we are now prepared for the drama and miracle of the Great Thanksgiving. This part of the service starts with the offertory.

THE OFFERTORY

Liturgical Life Principle 11: Things (material possessions) make us worry about the wrong things.

From the back of the church, the bread and wine are brought forward. In the early church and in some churches today, a member of the community would have baked bread for this moment in the service. The priest takes the basics of life to create a gift from God that can transform life; the bread, given as a gift, is used by God. As we move from the Word to the Sacrament, the focus is giving.

The truth about being human is that all we have, all we are, all we ever will be are gifts from God. At this moment we give back to God. Learning to give is a vitally important part of healthy and authentic living. Charles Dickens's famous story *The Christmas Carol* well captures a life damaged by selfishness. Ebenezer Scrooge is unable to see beyond himself: he refuses to see any need or even value in others. As a result he lives a desperately lonely life, which turns the accumulation of wealth into an end in itself.

At this moment in the service we are invited to reflect on our attitude toward "things." We are constantly challenged in Scripture not to allow things to become our "god." In fact, the Gospel of Luke frequently exhorts us to give our possessions away. It is astonishing how easy it is to become so attached to things that it distorts our view of reality. Imagine a situation where a child running around a beautiful, well-furnished home knocks over a prized object, which then shatters into a thousand pieces. It is true that the object may be of sentimental or monetary value and perhaps irreplaceable. But from the viewpoint of the healthy and authentic living project, it is still a "thing," which is, before God, of no value compared to the child. To yell at the child, to sink into a deep depression, or to allow the moment to damage the rest of the evening or the week would be tragic. Or take another illustration. At a delightful restaurant with a group of friends celebrating a wedding anniversary, the waiter accidentally dribbles a little red wine on your new outfit. The angry words to the waiter, coupled with real distress about the new outfit being wrecked, destroy the evening. Or we return to our car in a parking lot and find that some inconsiderate driver has dented the car door and then driven away without leaving a note. We so easily lapse into depression or rage that preoccupies us and inflicts misery on those around us. In each of these cases things have assumed a disproportionate place in our lives. We make furniture, gadgets, clothes, and cars into the things that matter instead of friends and family. We allow problems with things to damage our relationships with those around us.

Another major problem with things is that they take considerable time to acquire and maintain. A large home normally comes with a large mortgage and large heating bills, which involve lots of time at the office to ensure that we have enough money to maintain our lifestyle. Most of us find that our younger days, when all our possessions fit in a backpack, were much easier. It was always possible to take an afternoon off just to enjoy a warm summer day with friends. But once we are on the "things" escalator, we find all of life is focused on keeping these things up and running.

One can understand the instruction of Jesus that it is best not to have anything. The rich young ruler in Luke 18 is told by Jesus: "Sell everything you have and give to the poor, and you will have treasure in heaven. Then come, follow me" (Luke 18:22). If we don't have anything, then we can focus all our being on what really matters. If we are not constantly at the office we don't have to neglect our child. If we don't have a new car, we cannot get upset when it is damaged.

If we are going to have things (and, yes, the author has lots), then we are required to make sure that our possessions do not distort our values. It is at this moment in the service that we symbolically recommit to focusing on what matters. We do that by making a substantial gift. All giving should be a stretch, and we want to be sure that human lives are given priority over the new pair of shoes or the sixty-inch plasma television.

A healthy life is one where we make sure that our propensity to shop is kept in check. We should never allow things to matter so much that they assume a disproportionate status in our affections. As we write out the check for the offertory plate, we should remind ourselves of what matters much more than things. And we should give God thanks and praise for the health of friends and family and the gift of life for another day.

+ **For meditation:** Reflect on those moments when you worried too much about a "thing." Make a renewed commitment to try to live with less, freeing you up to give to those in need.

SURSUM CORDA
(LIFT UP YOUR HEARTS)

Liturgical Life Principle 12: Be grateful for all the things we simply assume.

The people remain standing. The Celebrant, whether bishop or priest, faces them and sings or says

	The Lord be with you.
People	And also with you.
Celebrant	Lift up your hearts.
People	We lift them to the Lord.
Celebrant	Let us give thanks to the Lord our God.
People	It is right to give him thanks and praise.

[BCP p. 361]

+ + +

The word "Eucharist" means thanksgiving, and the prayer that the priest now embarks on is called "The Great Thanksgiving." The prayer is introduced by a dialogue, known as the Sursum Corda (Lift up your hearts): the priest and the people are working on this together. We exchange the greeting; once again we ask the Creator of everything that is to come upon this endeavor. We lift up our hearts so our spirits connect with the Divine. And we enter into the "hymn" of thanksgiving, which tells the story of how in countless ways God has provided and we have been recklessly stubborn.

As we ease into the Great Thanksgiving, we are reminded of the importance of a life lived with a sense of gratitude. Many of us assume a baseline that we don't think about until that baseline is challenged. So we assume that we will be healthy, have sufficient food, enjoy a happy marriage, have healthy children, and have a good job. We start being grateful only when we receive something over and above these basics — like winning the lottery or finding time to have a dream vacation. The net result is that many of us are constantly dissatisfied. We become obsessed with what "we do not have" — a particular model of car or a palatial home.

One paradox of tragedy is that suddenly we are reminded of how infinitely precious food, health, and employment are. It's that moment when our child is in a hospital that suddenly we see what really matters. Our lack of gratitude for all those moments that our child was well is exposed, and the constant dream for an Audi R8 is replaced with the more vital and much more appropriate hope for healing. Sometimes we are so limited that it is only tragedy that can make us see what really matters. It's when a marriage is about to disintegrate because of neglect that we suddenly appreciate our spouse; it is when our body starts to deteriorate that we appreciate our health. It's when we are facing unemployment that we are suddenly grateful for the privilege of work (about which we constantly complain).

The Great Thanksgiving tells the story of God's constant pleas to humanity to recognize what matters. The climax of the narrative is the moment that God in Christ is a tragic victim of betrayal and pain and dies at the hands of God's creation. We are challenged in this prayer to recognize what really matters. For those who are coping with suffering, pain, and loss, we are invited to recognize how God can use this moment. As God did in Christ, so God can do in our lives. Those of us who are healthy, happy, and employed should bow the knee and thank God for the many blessings in our life.

The goal here is to be habitually grateful. We start every morning grateful for the fact that we have been granted another day of life.

As we sit near those who love us, we are grateful for the companionship. As we worry about our children, we are grateful for their energy, vitality, and, hopefully, growing virtue. As we glance out a window and see the sun setting, we marvel at the moment of sheer beauty. As we watch the snow fall and cover the world in breathtaking white, we are grateful for the diversity and movement of the seasons.

Gratitude does not require more than the countless miracles that impact every life every moment of every day. We don't need an Audi R8 to be grateful. In fact to imagine that an Audi R8 is important is completely distorted. Deep down we know that the privilege of love and laughter is much more important than the Audi R8.

As we work through this prayer, we are invited to cultivate a disposition of gratitude. We need to learn to be grateful to God for everything that God has done for us. God has made us, loved us, redeemed us, and provided for us. Even when everything is falling apart in our lives, God has still made us, loved us, redeemed us, and provided for us.

God does not promise us immortality. We are not going to live forever. Ultimately all of us will die. As we face this inevitability, we can react in one of two ways: we can become bitter and resentful or we can remain grateful for the life still left to us. Participation in the Great Thanksgiving cultivates the second response. Suffering is part of life. Suffering is the vehicle by which God will redeem the world. We recognize this reality and learn to work with it.

◆ **For meditation:** List everything you are thankful for—starting with the most basic and obvious (breath, eyesight) and move to the remarkable and particular (children, friendship). Say thank you to God.

SANCTUS

Liturgical Life Principle 13: Others have gone before; we are in good company.

Therefore we praise you, joining our voices with Angels and Archangels and with all the company of heaven, who for ever sing this hymn to proclaim the glory of your Name:

Celebrant and People

>Holy, holy, holy Lord, God of power and might,
>heaven and earth are full of your glory.
>   Hosanna in the highest.
>Blessed is he who comes in the name of the Lord.
>   Hosanna in the highest.   [BCP p. 362]

◆ ◆ ◆

As the priest works through the drama, we are invited to join with angels and archangels and with all the company of heaven to sing this song of praise.

It is worth pausing to meditate for a moment on the distinguished company. Participating in this "work of the people" (the literal meaning of the word "liturgy") is exciting work. Liturgy is a cosmic activity. To the modern Western mind, angels and archangels sound rather quaint and improbable, but there are no good reasons to be skeptical. God has created many different forms of being — lots of different plants, animals, and humans (we know about these because we are living among them). It is probable that there is life on other planets (and that life is probably very diverse). And on the basis of "revelation" (namely, that God has been revealed to the church in Scripture), we affirm that God has created entities that are in heaven.

The angels are in the work of worship with the communion of saints. The communion of saints represents an important challenge to our normal individualistic assumptions. We tend to assume that we face challenges alone and that no one understands or quite shares what we are going through. The communion of saints makes clear that there are plenty of people, who were once mortal, who completely understand what we are going through. At the very least these lives are an example to us; they can inspire and help us. In addition, as our Roman Catholic friends teach us, we can ask the saints to pray for us. After all, in the Episcopal burial service we find these words:

>O God, the King of saints, we praise and magnify thy holy Name for all thy servants who have finished their course in thy faith and fear; for the blessed Virgin Mary; for the holy patriarchs, prophets, apostles, and martyrs; and for all other thy righteous servants, known to us and unknown; and we beseech thee that, encouraged by their examples, aided by their

prayers, and strengthened by their fellowship, we also may be partakers of the inheritance of the saints in light; through the merits of thy Son Jesus Christ our Lord. Amen.

Modern living can easily make us feel alone. We are often miles away from our extended family. At this point in the liturgy, we are suddenly reminded of the "great cloud of witnesses" (Heb. 12:1) that surrounds us — our eternal extended family. We are not alone in our struggle to cope. Along with the transforming help of God, there are the angels and the saints there to support us in this exciting yet demanding project of living as God always intended.

♦ **For meditation:** Reflect on the lives of those you know who have gone before. If you feel comfortable doing so, ask a saint to pray for you.

Liturgical Life Principle 14: Even though people can be wickedly fickle, God is constantly willing to work on their lives.

Celebrant and People

Blessed is he who comes in the name of the Lord.
  Hosanna in the highest.   [BCP p. 362]

♦ ♦ ♦

The Sanctus (which means "holy") is an opportunity to offer God worship (revisiting a theme already identified under the description of the Gloria); however, the phrase "Blessed is he who comes in the name of the Lord, Hosanna in the highest" offers a new dimension to the healthy and authentic living project.

This phrase comes from the triumphant arrival of Jesus in Jerusalem on Palm Sunday. As we utter these words, we find ourselves remembering the events of that week. The crowd that celebrates Jesus on what we call Palm Sunday joins the crowd that called for his crucifixion on Good Friday. It is not surprising that as this part of the service begins many Christians cross themselves. We do so suddenly aware of how a worshiping throng one day can the next day become a mob encouraging the Romans to crucify goodness. People can be sincerely good on one day and say incredibly destructive things on the next.

Suddenly the liturgy becomes a challenge. God loves us despite ourselves. As we encounter opportunities to be cruel or unjust, God constantly challenges us and loves us through it all. The words spoken on Palm Sunday are still part of our liturgy. God wants to work with us to enable us to live as God intended. There is no giving up on us even though deep within us all there lies a deeply destructive potential.

> **The Sanctus** comes from the words of the seraphim in Isaiah 6:1–3. It was used in the synagogue liturgy, and we find it in Christian liturgies since the fourth century.
>
> **Benedictus qui venit.** As Jesus entered Jerusalem the people cried out, "Blessed is he who comes in the name of the Lord" (Matt. 21:9). The appearance of this passage in the liturgy goes back to 380 C.E. It was attached to the Sanctus in Gaul and later in Rome.

The fickleness of humanity is suddenly exposed. We can worship one day and behave in wicked ways the next. We can soar with angels at the start of the Sanctus and become a mob braying for blood moments later. God's intent remains steadfast through it all. God is there to transform us, by divine grace to make the moments of destructive wickedness an impossibility. Through the habit of participating in worship, God will help us to realize our potential for love and learn to challenge and transform our propensities for wickedness. We can be different. God wants to make us so.

+ **For meditation:** Recall those moments when you joined a crowd and were cruel to another person. Repent of that moment and make a commitment always to be willing to challenge the mob.

WORDS OF CONSECRATION

Liturgical Life Principle 15: In moments of betrayal, pain, and death, authentic living is made possible.

> *At the following words concerning the bread, the Celebrant is to hold it, or lay a hand upon it; and at the words concerning the cup, to hold*

or place a hand upon the cup and any other vessel containing wine to be consecrated.

On the night he was handed over to suffering and death, our Lord Jesus Christ took bread; and when he had given thanks to you, he broke it, and gave it to his disciples, and said, "Take, eat: This is my Body, which is given for you. Do this for the remembrance of me."

After supper he took the cup of wine; and when he had given thanks, he gave it to them, and said, "Drink this, all of you: This is my Blood of the new Covenant, which is shed for you and for many for the forgiveness of sins. Whenever you drink it, do this for the remembrance of me." [BCP pp. 362–63]

◆ ◆ ◆

It is inevitable: there are bound to be moments in our life when we stand before God devastated and distraught. All lives end in death.

The Episcopal liturgy invites us to face this reality every week. Death and suffering are not evaded, but faced as realities that need to be recognized. They are, however, faced in a way that is deeply poignant and ultimately triumphant. As we work through the Great Thanksgiving, we reenact the Last Supper. It is poignant because it is the last meal with friends "on the night he was handed over to suffering and death." Jesus gathers with those who are closest to him. He knows that he does not have long, so he blesses the bread and wine and shares the food with his friends. This moment is ultimately triumphant because it enables us to live life to the full — to live as God intended.

Both the poignancy and the triumph are recognized. As we grow older we recognize the reality of our own mortality. We become more sensitive to the fact that there are fewer times we will meet with friends. We become aware that the years are rolling by, and there will be fewer vacations with the grandchildren. One paradox of healthy living is that we develop a constructive attitude toward death. Death is rarely kind: it can come in shockingly unexpected ways. Usually we do not know that this is the last time we will see this or that friend. We are not always granted closure. So we should live life aware of the gift of the moment and the obligation to live in relationship with each other, aware of the possibility of death. In other words, at a very practical level we should not "let the sun go down on our wrath." It is unhealthy to allow a day to go by without the resolution of an argument. It is unhealthy to go for months or years alienated from a sibling or a child. We need to live life so that if the tragic occurs the tragic is not multiplied by our inability to have lived constructively with another. In other words, we don't want to experience the tragic death of a loved one with whom we had an argument but now no longer have the chance to heal the rift. If we live life aware of death, then we live it in such a way that we seek to heal divisions quickly. And we strive to make sure that our conscience is clear when we face the reality of mortality in this life.

At the time of this dinner with his friends, Jesus was a young man — only thirty-three. This was all happening during the Jewish season of Passover, although we are not sure whether it was a Seder meal (there is a lot of debate about this). He had brought life and hope to countless lives. He could feel the Roman authorities closing in on him as he sat and ate his last meal with friends. At this moment in the Eucharist, we are invited to participate, to join the meal. We are invited to be present. It is an important moment in the service. It is vitally important that on the eve of our death (whenever that might be), we are able to sit with those we love. We should examine our lives and challenge ourselves afresh not only to reach out to those who are unhappy with us but also appreciate those who are part of our lives each and every day.

The triumph of this moment is made possible by the miracle of God's grace in allowing Jesus Christ, God Incarnate, to die to enable us to live. This is the complex concept of atonement. Atonement means literally at-one-ment (God has made us one through the redeeming work of Christ). The church very wisely never made an official commitment to a particular view of the atonement. Scripture offers a variety of images: Jesus' death is a ransom, a sacrifice, an example, a victory. We are invited to affirm that this moment when Jesus, who is God Almighty, died at the hands of creation is a moment that changed the world and created fresh cosmic possibilities.

One way of understanding this moment is to recognize that God's participation in human life and suffering gives God the moral authority to forgive. Forgiveness is puzzling. How can God forgive the sins that one person has committed against another? I cannot forgive the sin of stealing committed by John against Mary (because

I am not Mary and therefore I haven't been wronged), so how can God forgive John?

The Christian answer is that God can forgive because God has been at the receiving end of pain, suffering, betrayal, and misunderstanding. An example might help: when Nelson Mandela was released from prison, he asked his fellow black South Africans not to take revenge on the whites, but rather to commit to living in harmony with them. He asked, in effect, for the black South Africans to forgive the whites for the years of domination and racism. He had the authority to forgive because he had spent the best years of his life locked in a prison cell on Robben Island. He had been a victim of the racist regime as much as any other black person in South Africa.

Christians believe that the presence of the Eternal Word of God in the life, death, and resurrection of Jesus gives God the "moral" authority to forgive all sin. And this solves a practical problem: often those we need forgiveness from are no longer around to forgive us. Through the sacrifice of Jesus on the cross we are now able to go to God and seek forgiveness. The cross shows us that God has been present in all suffering; it shows us that God has entered into suffering and tasted the despair and loneliness of death. So we are invited to seize the cross and know that we are forgiven.

Forgiveness eradicates the impact of the past. So many of us are coping with failure and hurt from the past that continues to haunt the present. The fact that we are forgiven by God means that we are fully restored. We are invited to enjoy the present free from the burden of coping with the confusion and muddle of our past.

So we have poignancy (as Jesus eats supper with his friends for the last time) and triumph (because in his death we know we are forgiven).

◆ **For meditation:** Reflect with thanksgiving on the life of Jesus given for humanity. Reflect as well on the tragedy of a life cut short.

THE ACCLAMATION

Liturgical Life Principle 16: When life is difficult, we should remember that we are all part of a cosmic drama that receives the love of God in Christ.

Therefore we proclaim the mystery of faith:

Celebrant and People

Christ has died.
Christ is risen.
Christ will come again.   [BCP p. 363]

❖ ❖ ❖

Life can be difficult. It can be difficult to believe that love and goodness will ultimately triumph over hatred and evil. But in this acclamation of our faith — Christ has died, Christ is risen, Christ will come again — we are invited to affirm this reality.

This is the moment when we cry out that the impression given by the nightly television news is wrong: evil and hatred are not going to triumph in this world. Staying in touch with our complicated world can be exhausting. We do so because we believe that we have a moral obligation to be informed. But this does mean that we are constantly in touch with broken lives scattered in communities around the globe.

The healthy and authentic living project requires that we place this misery and pain in some context. One dimension of our context is that the television news does not report the mundane, unchanging routine of most people's lives. "News," by definition, reports the spectacular, which is often tragic. But remember that there are plenty of good and happy occurrences every day that go unreported.

A larger context is stressed in the acclamation. Here is a summary of the cosmic engagement with humanity through Christ. Christ has been broken; Christ has died. We start there. However, this is not the end. Christ is risen. Christ has triumphed over death. The death of Christ captures the challenge of sin; the resurrection of Christ captures his victory over sin. Even though Christ has risen, evil and sinfulness continue to exist in our world. So the third affirmation comes to the fore: Christ will come again.

This is the Christian hope. We are forbidden to despair. Ultimately, God is in control. And ultimately God will ensure that love triumphs. This is what is meant by the affirmation that Christ will come again. The triumph over death will be totally realized throughout the universe. At some point in the future, God will step into history and ensure the triumph over hatred and selfishness.

So when we are tempted to despair about the world around us, perhaps when tragedy touches our lives, this moment in the service insists that we need to place our difficulties in an appropriate context, a context in which we acclaim that God has encountered suffering and ultimately love will triumph.

+ **For meditation:** The next time you watch the television news or read the newspaper, offer up prayers for the difficulties facing certain individuals, communities, and nations. And thank God that there is a guarantee of a triumph of love in Christ.

EPICLESIS

Liturgical Life Principle 17: There is a moment of divine grace found in the miracle of the sacrament that makes all the difference to our living.

Celebrant

Sanctify them by your Holy Spirit to be for your people the Body and Blood of your Son, the holy food and drink of new and unending life in him.   [BCP p. 363]

◆ ◆ ◆

At this point in the service a transforming resource of divine grace is made available. It is called the epiclesis, which means "invocation." Episcopalians believe that the priest is a channel of divine power to make God present in a distinctive and miraculous way. Along with Roman Catholics, Orthodox, and Lutherans, Episcopalians believe that all priests are in apostolic succession (in other words, through the agency of the Holy Spirit we are connected to the disciples of Jesus who were commissioned by Jesus to further the reign of God). The priest has the authority to make Christ present in the Eucharist. At this point, confusion abounds. So let us make clear precisely what happens and what does not happen. To understand what happens we need to understand the Christian doctrines of the Trinity and the Incarnation, which we will look at now.

Christians discovered early on that it was insufficient to work with one image of God. We inherited from Judaism the term "Father" to capture the greatness of the Creator (the aspect of God that underpins everything that is). We also used the term "Spirit" (the aspect of God that makes God present to us now). The crucial step for Christians is that they trusted the witness of the early disciples, who believed that in the life, death, and resurrection of Jesus, they had encountered God.

It is the triune experience of God as Creator, Eternal Word, and continuing presence that caused Christians to start talking about God as Triune. God, they argued, needs to be understood as a Trinity. God is one (absolutely and definitely) but is disclosed to us in three ways (as Creator, Revealer, and Sanctifier). The Father is the biblical name for the aspect of God that creates. The second person of the Trinity — the Son, the Eternal Word — completely interpenetrated the life of Jesus of Nazareth. This means that when we look at the life of Jesus, we see a complete disclosure of what God is like. This disclosure includes the brokenness of God on the cross, crucified by creation. We see God's participation in the "hell" and "pain" of death at the hands of brutal power. The mystery of the sacrament connects with this moment in human history and is made possible by the triune God at this moment in the Eucharistic prayer.

> **Epiclesis.** We find in the third century liturgies that call on the Holy Spirit. From the fourth century onward, the Eastern church invokes the Spirit to be poured out on the congregation and the gifts.

We address God the Father. We address the Creator of everything that is — God in God's vastness, who made every planet and solar system. We ask the Father to send the Holy Spirit — the aspect of God that makes God present to us today. And the work of the Holy Spirit is to allow the Eternal Word to enter the elements (the bread and wine) and enable them to be the "Body and Blood of your Son."

Now it is true that if you put the bread and the wine under a microscope, you will see no difference before and after this prayer. The elements remain bread and wine. However, such reductionism is silly: it is also true that if you reduce people to their component parts all you find is lots of water and a bundle of chemicals. A true account of anything is more than the sum of its parts. When my father used to make bread at home, on one level it was just the ingredients that he put together and then placed in the oven. But on another level, it was bread made to be eaten in a family meal at the table. The truth of what these ingredients were must include the fact that it was bread made to be eaten.

At this moment of the service, there is a mystery of divine grace in operation. The priest is using these ingredients in a distinctive way. This is no longer just bread and wine. These elements have been interpenetrated by the second person of the Trinity. At this moment we are touching Christ. We are holding an energy that we can take into our lives: we are being given the promise of God that we too can be Christlike.

This is an amazing moment in the service. Throughout this book many of the moments in the service have been opportunities to think afresh about our lives and our values. At this moment God steps in. God wants to do the hard work of transforming us. We are not obligated to transform ourselves by our own efforts, but we are invited to seize on the resource that God wants to provide. The Creator of the universe provides a gift that can help us to live as God always intended.

So we eat and drink: we take Jesus into us. We receive the bread and wine knowing that they are an enormous resource. We are now empowered by a fuel that God has provided.

+ **For meditation:** Every week we witness the miracle of the Holy Eucharist. Focus on this miracle and thank God for it.

THE LORD'S PRAYER

Liturgical Life Principle 18: If we let God transform us, then we will start wanting and praying for the things that God wants us to have.

And now, as our Savior Christ has taught us, we are bold to say,	As our Savior Christ has taught us, we now pray,

People and Celebrant

Our Father, who art in heaven, hallowed be thy Name, thy kingdom come, thy will be done, on earth as it is in heaven. Give us this day our daily bread.	Our Father in heaven, hallowed be your Name, your kingdom come, your will be done, on earth as in heaven. Give us today our daily bread.

And forgive us our trespasses,
   as we forgive those
     who trespass against us.
And lead us not into temptation,
   but deliver us from evil.
For thine is the kingdom,
   and the power, and the glory,
   for ever and ever. Amen.
	Forgive us our sins
	   as we forgive those
	     who sin against us.
	Save us from the time of trial,
	   and deliver us from evil.
	For the kingdom, the power,
	   and the glory are yours,
	   now and for ever. Amen.
	[BCP pp. 363–64]

It is because of everything that God has done that the priest announces that we are "bold to say" the Lord's Prayer. We are now ready to say the prayer that Jesus gave his disciples when they asked him, "Lord, teach us to pray." A sense of history helps us to appreciate this moment: we utter words that were originally spoken by Jesus and captured in the Gospels. These words, two thousand years old, connect us with the definitive disclosure of God in history.

As we connect with Jesus, we are invited to recognize that the life that God intended us to live is one in which we learn to value God's expectations for our lives and world. The prayer begins with the privilege of approaching God as Father. We are invited to see God as a parent who loves and cares for us. At the same time, we are also reminded that God is holy. We see God as intimate yet transcendent, as a friend yet the Creator of everything that is.

The Lord's Prayer moves to the reign of God: thy kingdom come. Ultimately we want everything to be rightly ordered. We want everything to be surrounded by love and justice. As we pray for the coming of the kingdom, we remind ourselves of the importance of our contribution to bringing about God's reign. We have an obligation to play our part. The place to start is in our lives. The goal of the entire liturgy is to allow God to be sovereign in our life. And as we are transformed we begin to transform the communities we are in.

Three petitions follow. First, "Give us our daily bread." We do need our "daily bread," the basics of life. It is perfectly proper to ask for this basic provision. Second, "Forgive us our sins." We need to receive forgiveness and, at the same time, give forgiveness. Forgiveness is the powerhouse of a changed life. Living with unforgiven hatred and animosity leads to a haunted and tragic life; forgiving a past wrong frees us up to live for the present. Knowing that our weaknesses and failures are forgiven by God is also a moment of liberation. The past cannot be changed. While we can regret our actions and have to live with their consequences, we can also know that our Creator forgives us. As far as God is concerned, it is a new day. We are not obligated to be captive to our past. We free ourselves by forgiving others; and we are freed by God and by God's forgiveness. The third petition is "save us from the time of trial" and "deliver us from evil." Evil can capture human lives. In this petition, we ask for the power of God to resist the forces of evil that are present in our lives. Evil is often at its strongest when love is about to triumph.

The prayer ends where it begins, with the words of worship: "for thine is the kingdom, the power, and the glory." We acknowledge who God is. In so doing, we celebrate the privilege of prayer and set our priorities accordingly. To what extent are we reflecting in our lives God's values? To what extent are we loving and good rather than egotistical and selfish? The challenge of the healthy and authentic living project is brought home once again at the end of the Lord's Prayer.

◆ **For meditation:** Reflect on the balance between worship and petitions. Marvel at how these are balanced in this prayer.

THE FRACTION

Liturgical Life Principle 19: Brokenness can be the key to life.

The Celebrant breaks the consecrated Bread.

A period of silence is kept.

Then may be sung or said

[Alleluia.] Christ our Passover is sacrificed for us;
Therefore let us keep the feast. [Alleluia.]

In Lent, Alleluia is omitted, and may be omitted at other times except during Easter Season.

In place of, or in addition to, the preceding, some other suitable anthem may be used. [BCP p. 364]

◆ ◆ ◆

Immediately prior to the distribution, there is a moment of extraordinary drama. The consecrated bread is broken, and in response the congregation recognizes the miracle of this moment in what is called "the fraction."

At this point in the service we are invited to participate in a paradox: a broken life can be the key to wholeness or, another way of putting it, a life sacrificed can be the key to life for others. We might be tempted to think that nothing good can come from the powerful crushing the powerless, from an innocent man being found guilty. But through the agency of God's grace, we are invited to see that everything good can come from such moments. God can take the tragic and make it a resource for wholeness.

Grace in brokenness is a key theme of the Gospel. But we can also see it working in our own lives. To take one illustration, my mother died when I was seventeen. The year before she died was also the year I had to take the exams that would enable me to attend the university. For various complex reasons, I did not do well in the exams. In July I received the news that I would not be able to go to the university of my choice and would have to wait a year and retake the examinations. I was devastated. Preoccupied with my pain and disappointment, I went to see my mother, who at this point was only three months away from death. As she lay there in her own brokenness and pain, she held her son close to her, shared fully my crushing disappointment, and entirely understood my self-absorbed hurt. This was a moment of divine grace in brokenness. This was a moment in which my mother transcended her own pain to reach out and identify with the disappointment of her son. The miracle was in her capacity to love through the tragedy of the cancer that was destroying her body. For all sorts of understandable reasons, illness makes a person turn within — bitter, alienated, and unable to reach out. In an act of divine grace my mother transcended her brokenness to bring love to her son (who was ironically too self-absorbed to see how trivial his disappointment was). Her act has remained with me and become an integral part of my understanding of the world.

In Jesus we have a broken body, a body crucified. It is this body that brings the world redemption. Through the paradox of persecution and crucifixion we have God's grace.

+ **For meditation:** Reflect on moments in your life when you have seen people transcend their brokenness and bring grace to others.

POSTCOMMUNION PRAYER

Liturgical Life Principle 20: This service has made a difference. Equipped and ready we can live a changed life.

After Communion, the Celebrant says

Let us pray.

Celebrant and People

Eternal God, heavenly Father,
you have graciously accepted us as living members
of your Son our Savior Jesus Christ,
and you have fed us with spiritual food
in the Sacrament of his Body and Blood.
Send us now into the world in peace,
and grant us strength and courage
to love and serve you
with gladness and singleness of heart;
through Christ our Lord. Amen.   [BCP p. 365]

◆ ◆ ◆

Almost all self-help books require lots of effort on the part of the reader. The secret, the books explain, is a positive attitude. "Don't let your low self-esteem trap you," they exhort. It is all up to us to make the difference. As we come toward the end of this service, the twentieth Liturgical Life Principle states that our simple participation in this service has already done some good. The sacrament that we have received is a resource from God for our healthy and authentic living project. The prayers we have participated in really do create options that would not have been there without our prayers.

In this postcommunion prayer, we recognize what we have received and acknowledge the difference that the sacrament makes. We are now ready to go out "into the world in peace." This prayer really captures what the healthy and authentic living project involves. It all comes down to this: "love and service with gladness and singleness of heart." And it is worth breaking down this phrase and examining it with some care.

Let us start with the words "love" and "service." These two words are often misunderstood. We shouldn't confuse this kind of love with a delightful romantic obsession with another person. It is also important to distinguish this love from sexual desire. Instead, love here refers to giving ourselves to others in service. Love and service are intrinsically linked. This giving of ourselves to others, however, should not be called "self-giving." Sometimes Christians talk about the obligation to "give completely of ourselves to others in service." This is misleading. If we gave *completely,* then there wouldn't be a self from which to love. We are not called to be doormats in the service of others. This sort of theology of "love" has been deeply damaging, especially to women. There are many women who have dedicated their lives to serving others: inconsiderate husbands, demanding children, needy parents. But self-care is an important Christian obligation, and it means that we construct healthy, mutually sustaining relationships that enhance life for everyone.

The disposition underpinning love and service are "gladness and singleness of heart." We are not called to serve others resentfully or unhappily; we are called to serve with joy and focus. How we serve is a vitally important part of the healthy and authentic living project. Service rendered out of duty or obligation can make us feel resentful. If we can find joy in our service, then the service can bring us joy. We do damage to ourselves if we engage our duties with resentment that corrodes the spirit. It destroys the effectiveness of the service.

Finding joy and focus expressed in love and service is our prayer here. It is a beautiful prayer that prepares us to step into the world confident that God has done a little more work on our lives.

* **For meditation:** Do we serve resentfully or with "gladness"? Reflect on the difference between the two.

THE BLESSING

Liturgical Life Principle 21: We are guaranteed the presence of God during the struggles of the next week.

The blessing of God Almighty, the Father, the Son, and the Holy Spirit, be upon you and remain with you for ever. *Amen.*

[BCP p. 339]

◆ ◆ ◆

In Episcopal theology the priest is a channel of divine blessing. Thanks to a connection between the priest standing in front of us in the church and the apostles who received the commission from Jesus himself, the priest has the authority to bring the blessing of God Almighty to the congregation.

There is a beauty in this moment. We receive the blessing perhaps by crossing ourselves. Making of the sign of the cross is an ancient Christian practice. First and foremost it is a reminder of the sacrament of baptism. We were baptized using the Trinitarian formula and the sign of the cross to seal us as Christ's own. Second, it is a recognition that we live under the authority of the cross. Who we are and what we are have been made possible by the work of divine grace on the cross. Once again we are touching on the deep paradox that in the moment of divine weakness — as Jesus died on the cross — we see divine power. In that moment of total and complete love for the world, we see God create completely new possibilities for the future of the cosmos. Given that much of human life is coping with suffering, the sign of the cross represents a powerful recognition that suffering is the basis of our redemption. Third, the sign of the cross can be a prayer to God. As we touch our forehead, we ask that God be present in our mind; as we touch our stomach or chest, we ask that God be in our bodies; as we touch our shoulders, we ask that God be in everything we do. We want love to permeate our being. We want to live a transformed life enabled by God. We want to leave this service equipped to serve God more effectively.

♦ **For meditation:** We receive the blessing of God through our sense of truth. Reflect on how we are called to serve God using all our senses — our entire body.

Chapter Five

Living Every Day in Gratitude

A weekly reorientation toward God is vitally important. It needs to be done with fellow travelers. We all struggle with egotism and destructive tendencies; the act of standing alongside each other helps us to support each other in the hard work of the healthy and authentic living project.

The encounter in corporate worship every Sunday is a vital part of the project, but it needs to be supplemented by daily discipline. The idea of daily discipline has fallen out of fashion among many Christians. We can learn something at this point from our Muslim friends. When I was the dean of Hartford Seminary (which is one-third Muslim), I learned to admire and appreciate the daily discipline of prayer that pervades the life of observant Muslims. These five obligatory prayer times assure that the day is interrupted by the important reminder that God exists. As a Muslim friend of mine observed, too often Episcopalians live like atheists. We live as if God doesn't exist. We don't think about God during the busy and hectic day. In so doing, we seriously impede the healthy and authentic living project. It is a bit like the person on a diet who seriously watches calories only one day a week and then wonders why the diet isn't successful.

Carving out some time each day for God can transform the day. We learn to live reflectively. There is a risk that in our twilight years we will wonder why we didn't appreciate more those moments when we were young and carefree or savor the years when our children were growing up. By pausing for God, we pause for everything else. We consciously recall our good health, the fun moments, our children in prayer; we consciously offer our employment concerns to God; and we consciously relish the moments of living.

Starting a daily practice can be difficult. For some Episcopalians, the very image of spending time with God every day is a problem.

It is associated with fundamentalist religion. Episcopalians pride themselves on not being too enthusiastic; after all, enthusiastic religion can lead to dangerous extremes of intolerance. But spending time with God should not lead to intolerance. Indeed an encounter with cosmic love should have the opposite effect; it should lead to the cultivation of a disposition of generosity and understanding.

The prayer book provides daily devotions for individuals and families. It suggest four moments during the day when we should pause and remember God. In this chapter we will focus on the start and the end of the day. These daily devotions provide a powerful means of continuing the work that starts on Sunday. Beginning with the Morning and Evening devotions can be a realistic way to begin the work of a daily discipline of prayer.

IN THE MORNING

From Psalm 51

Open my lips, O Lord, *
  and my mouth shall proclaim your praise.
Create in me a clean heart, O God, *
  and renew a right spirit within me.
Cast me not away from your presence *
  and take not your holy Spirit from me.
Give me the joy of your saving help again *
  and sustain me with your bountiful Spirit.
Glory to the Father, and to the Son, and to the Holy Spirit: *
  as it was in the beginning, is now, and will be for ever. Amen.

A Reading

Blessed be the God and Father of our Lord Jesus Christ! By his great mercy we have been born anew to a living hope through the resurrection of Jesus Christ from the dead.   *1 Peter 1:3*

A period of silence may follow.

A hymn or canticle may be used; the Apostles' Creed may be said.

Prayers may be offered for ourselves and others.

The Lord's Prayer

The Collect

Lord God, almighty and everlasting Father, you have brought us in safety to this new day: Preserve us with your mighty power, that we may not fall into sin, nor be overcome by adversity; and in all we do, direct us to the fulfilling of your purpose; through Jesus Christ our Lord. *Amen.*   [BCP p. 137]

◆ ◆ ◆

Psalm 51

Liturgical Life Principle 22: The past is past; we should give God the past and invite God to work in the present.

Starting the day with Psalm 51 means we start with a sense of penitence, with a sense that we continue to struggle in many ways. Destructive forces lie deep within us. It is so easy to lapse into patterns of behavior that damage those we love and others around us. It is so easy to become preoccupied with what we do not have that we fail to appreciate everything we have. It is so easy to dwell on our insecurities and anxieties so that we crush any joy out of the current moment. This psalm challenges us to shift our ground. We are going to live in this moment today and free ourselves from the destructive power of the past.

The psalm invites us to prepare for the gift of praising God. Once again we are reminded of how great it is to simply enjoy God for who God is. The Creator of everything that is wants us to start the day enjoying God's company. We invite God to deal with our past by creating a clean heart and a right spirit and by not taking the Holy Spirit from us. At this point we give God our past. We cannot do anything about the past. It sits there — an unalterable reality. The older we get the more likely it is that almost every day we offer back to God moments when we really messed up. These are moments when we made decisions that were damaging. Some destructive force overwhelmed us and led to a set of events that we regret. We are invited through this daily discipline to keep giving this back to God. God has the authority to forgive. God can create the fresh start.

Having surrendered the past to God, we are now able to focus on the present. This is a joyful present sustained by the Spirit of God. We are going to live this day differently. As a result of entering deeply into the words of this psalm, we are in a new place. The anxieties that haunt us from the past can be given back to God, and the power of God to transform the present is made available.

* **For meditation:** No one can do anything about the past. Reflect on those moments in the past that are continuing to haunt you and offer those moments to God.

The Reading

Liturgical Life Principle 23: Learning about God in the written Word creates a new horizon for human living.

Having prepared ourselves to spend some time with God, we now turn to the written Word. The service suggests a verse for meditation — a beautiful text from 1 Peter 1:3. Meditating on one verse can be very powerful. We are invited to concentrate and enjoy the language and explore the concepts very intentionally, arriving at a deep understanding of the words. Once we are familiar with this Scripture, we might want to choose others. A good source is the daily lectionary or "Forward Day by Day" or the Internet site "sacred space."[8]

In terms of the healthy and authentic living project, there is important work being done through daily meditation on the Bible. As we fill our minds with God we are less likely to fill our minds with destructive thoughts. Fortunately humans are limited. For example, when we really get into a great novel, we find ourselves totally absorbed by the world of the novel and not thinking about anything else. Likewise, the constructive engagement with the text of the Bible excludes a preoccupation with anything else.

Rather than spending hours poring over a glossy magazine, which causes dissatisfaction with our lifestyle, appearance, and attainments, we can spend time with the Bible to create a new horizon where our priorities are rightly ordered and our significance is appropriately affirmed. As the Apostle Paul puts it in Philippians, "Whatever is true, whatever is honorable, whatever is just, whatever is pure, whatever is lovely, whatever is gracious, if there is any excellence, if there is anything worthy of praise, think about these things" (Phil. 4:8). If we read Scripture carefully, we find ourselves thinking about Scripture. Thinking about Scripture means that we are not thinking about things that will lead us away from God. Suddenly, we are living in a different place — a place more healthy and life-enhancing.

This reading provides a thought that we will want to revisit during the day. It provides a resource and support for healthy and authentic living.

+ **For meditation:** What do you spend your time thinking about? Is this a healthy place or an unhealthy one?

Prayer and the Lord's Prayer

Liturgical Life Principle 24: Offer to God the details of your life.

In Sunday prayer our immediate worries are situated in the vast web of complexities of our modern world. We are suddenly reminded that our worries about our child's grades at school need to be located in a context in which some parents are worrying about the survival of their children in a war zone or with a famine looming. In bringing to God the concerns of others who really are facing greater problems, we situate our worries and are invited to place them in an appropriate perspective.

This is not to say that bringing our worries to God is inappropriate. God cares about all the details of our lives. From the trivial to the major, God cares. One reason it is important not to turn God into a big human person is that it is a little bizarre to imagine God as an invisible mind telepathically tuning into the 6 billion lives on planet Earth. Rather the image we need has God the sustainer of the universe enfolding and engaging with all our lives. It is because God is present at the enabling breath of every human being that God has intimate knowledge of everything we do, think, and say. Much like a novelist creates a universe for all her characters and knows those characters in all their complexities, so God as Creator is intimately involved with all our lives.

On a daily basis we are invited to bring all the details of our life to God. We are allowed to go to the deep places where we fear to tread. We are allowed to acknowledge our secret desires, fears, and anxieties. We are allowed to admit that we don't feel valued or appreciated. We are encouraged to admit that we are disappointed at where we find ourselves. It is so easy to be in denial. We deny our real feelings and fears. In the presence of God, there is no point in self-delusion because God knows the truth. As we are honest with God, so we will be honest with ourselves.

The act of offering prayer for ourselves and those near to us is itself deeply liberating. Everything that matters most in our lives is shared with God. Like all parents I worry about my son. The daily act of sharing my fears, hopes, and worries with God enables me to live that day confident that God is present with my son. Of course, I recognize that tragic things can happen. But I am also confident that even in some tragedy — God forbid — God will be present. When parents are away from a child, they worry. But it is physically impossible to be constantly present with our children. Our act of offering our child's life to God's care enables us to know that there is a presence surrounding our child.

When we are alone with God, we are allowed to be silly. To pray, for example, that the Yankees win the World Series is of course silly. God is placed in an impossible position: the Red Sox fans are all making the opposite prayer, and it is not obvious that the purposes of love are served by either team winning. In silence with God our deepest aspirations are allowed to surface. We are allowed to express our passion as a supporter of our team. As we live constantly in the space of daily prayer, we will learn increasingly to ask that "thy will be done." Slowly we will learn that we desire a universe where the purposes of love are realized and that seeking the realization of God's will is the route to such a universe.

This is the reason that this quiet, dedicated space with God always concludes with the Lord's Prayer. This is the prayer where the priorities are exactly right. And right in the middle of that prayer is the petition "Thy will be done on earth as it is in heaven." However silly our prayers might be as we confront the Divine with our confusion, questions, and struggling petitions, the Lord's Prayer ensures that we utter at least one appropriate prayer. Saying the Lord's Prayer every time we have dedicated time with God is a particular privilege and joy. We come out of our prayer moment conscious that we have uttered the words that Jesus spoke as a model prayer for all his disciples.

+ **For meditation:** Distinguish between the silly prayers and the important prayers. Offer both to God but recognize the difference.

The Collect

Liturgical Life Principle 25: Start the day with gratitude and hope.

The concluding collect is a complete delight, a prayer worth memorizing. We are starting a new day, so we rightly and appropriately thank God for the gift of the morning. Being grateful for simply being is a vital part of the healthy and authentic living project.

When we live with a sense of gratitude for the privilege of breathing, we are guaranteed a positive disposition. Most of us can add to the list. We are not simply breathing; we have arms, legs, people around us who love us, and a new opportunity to make a difference.

This opportunity to make a difference is the focus of the rest of the prayer. We ask the God of power to sustain us, support us, and enable us to live as God intended. We start the day with a sense that there are things to do. We cannot say this prayer and then crawl back into bed or waste the day. We finish the morning devotion ready to get going. Today we are going to serve the Almighty. This service might not command a massive salary or involve advanced technical skills. Because it is service to the Almighty, it is special. This is a day that we will give to God.

+ **For meditation:** Take out a sheet of paper and list everything you are grateful for.

AT THE CLOSE OF DAY

Psalm 134

Behold now, bless the LORD, all you servants of the LORD, *
    you that stand by night in the house of the LORD.
Lift up your hands in the holy place and bless the LORD; *
    the LORD who made heaven and earth bless you out of Zion.

A Reading

Lord, you are in the midst of us and we are called by your Name: Do not forsake us, O Lord our God. *Jer. 14:9, 22*

The following may be said

Lord, you now have set your servant free *
    to go in peace as you have promised;
For these eyes of mine have seen the Savior, *
    whom you have prepared for all the world to see:
A Light to enlighten the nations, *
    and the glory of your people Israel.

Prayers for ourselves and others may follow. It is appropriate that prayers of thanksgiving for the blessings of the day, and penitence for our sins, be included.

The Lord's Prayer

The Collect

Visit this place, O Lord, and drive far from it all snares of the enemy; let your holy angels dwell with us to preserve us in peace; and let your blessing be upon us always; through Jesus Christ our Lord. *Amen.*

The almighty and merciful Lord, Father, Son, and Holy Spirit, bless us and keep us. *Amen.*   [BCP p. 140]

◆ ◆ ◆

Psalm 134

Liturgical Life Principle 26: The values embodied in God should be affirmed constantly.

We start our brief meditation at the end of the day with a psalm of worship. The Westminster Shorter Catechism (a famous statement of belief from the Church of Scotland) states simply and boldly that our "chief end is to glorify God, and to enjoy him forever." As we have already seen, this means that we recognize in God those values that ultimately matter and are of ultimate worth. The goal of living is to focus our entire being on these values and to allow them to permeate our being. The result is the glorification and enjoyment of God.

We finish the day with our mind focused on what really matters. We finish the day full of the values of love, goodness, and justice. It is with this focus that we are going to look back at the day.

◆ **For meditation:** What do we consider important? Are the things we consider important of eternal value?

Nunc Dimmitis

Liturgical Life Principle 27: In our encounter with Jesus we have discovered everything that matters: if we are taken tomorrow, then we can go content.

It makes sense at the end of the day to reflect a little on our mortality and where we are in life. If I died tomorrow, what sense could be made of my life? This is the sort of question that people often face only when they are unhappy or disappointed with their life. However, with the Nunc Dimmitis (the opening words in Latin; it means "now you are dismissing"), we are invited to confront this question.

It is all triggered by this beautiful canticle (a canticle is a song found in Scripture used in the worship of the church). This canticle is taken from Luke 2 and is called the Song of Simeon. It is a delightful story of an old man (presumably) who reflects on his life in the light of encountering the child Jesus. The story is worth reproducing in full:

Now there was a man in Jerusalem whose name was Simeon; this man was righteous and devout, looking forward to the consolation of Israel, and the Holy Spirit rested on him. It had been revealed to him by the Holy Spirit that he would not see death before he had seen the Lord's Messiah. Guided by the Spirit, Simeon came into the temple; and when the parents brought in the child Jesus, to do for him what was customary under the law, Simeon took him in his arms and praised God, saying,

"Master, now you are dismissing your servant in peace,
    according to your word;
for my eyes have seen your salvation,
    which you have prepared in the presence of all peoples,
light for revelation to the Gentiles
    and for glory to your people Israel."

And the child's father and mother were amazed at what was being said about him. Then Simeon blessed them and said to his mother Mary, "This child is destined for the falling and the rising of many in Israel, and to be a sign that will be opposed so that the inner thoughts of many will be revealed — and a sword will pierce your own soul too." (Luke 2:25–35)

Simeon is here reflecting on his life, and in his encounter with the child Jesus he knows that he has encountered everything that matters. This is the joy of faith. In our encounter with the God revealed in Christ, we are entitled to have closure. Our life is guaranteed meaning, however tragic our ending might be. As we read the words of Simeon, we are invited to reflect on our life. Simeon recognizes in Jesus the revelation to the Gentiles and the glory to the

Jewish people. And as he holds Jesus in his arms, Simeon is ready to die. He is ready to be "dismissed in peace."

At this point, we are invited to reflect on our own lives. We are invited to see that however disappointed we might be that our ambitions have not been realized, we still have everything that matters. We are loved by God; we are redeemed through Christ; we are being sanctified by the Holy Spirit. We have encountered and been blessed by this child Jesus.

It is an important part of the healthy and authentic living project that we do not fear our death. Naturally, like most people, I desperately want to see my son grow up. But if this is not to be, then I must learn to rest content in the work that God has done in my life. This is Simeon's attitude and one that we all need to cultivate. A perfect end to a day is when we can say, "If I die this night, then I will have been blessed with everything that matters most."

◆ **For meditation:** How do you feel about death?

Concluding Collect

Liturgical Life Principle 28: God is our cosmic friend.

The last prayer of the day reminds us that God is our cosmic friend. A major theme of this book has been self-esteem. The lack of self-esteem is crippling. Some are terrified to assert themselves because of their lack of education and affirmation. We live in a very status-conscious world. People grade themselves on a hierarchy: they are especially conscious of those below and constantly aspire to be higher.

It is odd how the distinctions between people matter so much. From the divine perspective, they are silly. God is God: all human distinctions disappear from that vantage point. In fact, the Bible teaches us that children and the poor are the important ones. The Bible constantly turns the perception of the world upside down. God does not buy into the human perception of value and hierarchy.

At the end of the day, we invite God to visit us, protect us, and send God's holy angels to enable us to dwell in peace. God is our cosmic friend and comforter. Our last thought at the end of the day is a sense of affirmation. Regardless of how difficult our work is, the Creator of the universe is present with us.

◆ **For meditation:** Just enjoy the thought: you are special.

Chapter Six

How the History of the Prayer Book Contributes to the Healthy and Authentic Living Project

God has been here before. Tempting though it is to imagine that God has a unique set of problems with my particular life, it isn't true. God has been working on human lives for millennia. There is nothing in my life that God has not already seen. God is ready for every problem, difficulty, and challenge that my life can generate.

When we participate in an Episcopal service, we join a tradition. We are part of a chain that has its roots in the New Testament and will continue long after we are gone. The project is the same: the worship of God, enabled by Christ, facilitated by the Holy Spirit, to enable humans to become what God always intended: persons who are rightly ordered and radiating love to others. This human chain has been working on the liturgy project for centuries. Those living today are deeply indebted to the wisdom and richness of the liturgy that we inherit.

Why is this historical context of our liturgy so important? Its importance lies in the connection with other lives that have struggled with the challenge of egotism and the potential transformation of love. The historical sense of the millions upon millions of lives lived within a liturgical framework should bring a sense of reassurance. There will be moments when we are desperate. In those moments we reach out and celebrate the connection with countless lives that have gone before.

This historical sense is the best possible antidote to despair. Despair is a deep sin. We are forbidden to think that our life is not worth living. However complicated our life might be, we should always remain grateful for the simple gift of life, for the fact that we are starting this particular day with breath and consciousness. This basic gratitude is the foundation to healthy and authentic living. If we are living, then we have something to be grateful for.

There will be days when we are close to despair. We find ourselves with a broken heart due to the breakdown of a relationship. We find ourselves mourning others whom we love. We might be facing unemployment or losing our home. We might have credit card debt that is getting out of control. We might be prisoners to pornography, drugs, or alcohol. We might have destructive patterns of behavior that we cannot escape. As a result, we find ourselves just overwhelmed.

This is where the historical sense of the liturgy is so important. When we stand in a church (however small the congregation might be), we are connecting with millions of other people. And somewhere in those millions is a life on the cusp of despair — a life with problems like ours. As we think about this truth, we take comfort. We realize that these prayers provided the resources for others in similar situations to cope, and so we can use the same resources to cope with our problems.

Let us now embark on a very brief journey. This short survey of the history of the text that we hold in our hands every Sunday is no more than an introduction. At every point there are numerous complexities that could be discussed. The goal here is not to provide a comprehensive history, but to highlight certain themes in our history that should be part of the healthy and authentic living project.

Back to the New Testament

We know from the book of Acts that the Christians would meet regularly to attend the temple, break bread, and pray (Acts 2:42–46). It seems that right from the outset the Jewish practice of participating in daily prayers — morning and evening — was part of Christian practice. Participating in the "breaking the bread" is almost certainly a reference to a shared meal at which the Last Supper of Jesus is remembered. Christians would participate in this shared meal often — indeed, the Acts passage implies that it was daily (Acts 2:46). Many liturgical forms and practices in use today are taken from Scripture. Along with baptism and the Eucharist, we have the Lord's Prayer (Matt. 6:9–13 and Luke 11:2–4), prayers for healing

(James 5:14), confession of sins (James 5:16), and the laying on of hands (1 Tim. 4:14). When we participate in an Episcopal service, we are making a connection with the very origins of our faith.

The Early Church

It is amazing how soon formal liturgical texts began to appear. In the third century, we have the *Apostolic Tradition* of Hippolytus; in the middle of the fourth century, we find the Egyptian sacramentary of Serapion; and in the late fourth century, there is the *Apostolic Constitution,* which was developed in Asia Minor. Naturally different forms of liturgy emerged in different parts of the world. With the conversion of the Roman emperor Constantine, it became politically important to encourage liturgical unity, and so more liturgical texts started to appear. Two official liturgies became important: in the East the Liturgy of St. John Chrysostom and in the West the Roman Rite.

Problems

Like everything human, the development of liturgy had its own problems. Being aware of this should make us sensitive to the privilege of our own participation. Just as the opportunity to vote is valued when we understand how many people were denied that opportunity, so the privilege of participating in the Eucharist should be more greatly appreciated if we understand how the church went through periods when countless people were denied that opportunity.

The problems started with the fall of the Roman Empire. The theological focus was less on joy and more on penitence. In accord with the lay piety of the day, people started to stay away from the wine. After all, it was the blood of Jesus, and there were real fears of spilling it. Often it was only the priest who understood the words of the Mass because it was all in Latin. It became commonplace to receive the Eucharist only at Easter and just to be present at other times of the year. This was a low point of the church's liturgical life. We had traveled a long way from the daily "breaking of the bread" in Acts. We needed to recover a more positive liturgical disposition, one really focused on the healthy and authentic living project. There were good reasons for the Protestant Reformation.

The Anglican Reformation

In England, the Reformation took a particular form. Although there were many factors at work in the English Reformation, the trigger was the need for King Henry VIII — a deeply committed Roman Catholic — to receive an annulment. He rejected the authority of the pope yet wanted to maintain continuity with Catholic theology. So a tradition was born that located itself firmly between Geneva (the home of John Calvin and Reformed theology) and Rome (the home of the pope).

The English church was entirely comfortable in claiming as its own the rich liturgical resources of the Roman rite. On June 9, 1549, the English parliament created the first Book of Common Prayer. It was a *tour de force*. Archbishop Thomas Cranmer put it together drawing on material found in the Missal (a range of resources used primarily in monasteries), the Breviary (the prayers, psalms, and canticles needed for the Daily Office), the Manual (liturgies used for pastoral services, e.g., visiting the sick, marriage, and baptism), and the Pie (the rubrics [directions]) for the exercise of these liturgies). Cranmer's selection was inspired (literally, so I believe, by the Holy Spirit). His translations from Latin to English were elegant and powerful.

This was a difficult time for the church. Conservatives wanted the Latin back: the progressives wanted the theology to be much more reformed. A more reformed prayer book emerged under Queen Elizabeth I. Yet this edition was itself revised under King Charles II in 1662. It is this edition that became the basis for every prayer book in the Anglican world. This prayer book makes clear that the Anglican tradition is located midway between the Presbyterians and the Catholic high church party. The Anglican tradition is an ecumenical project.[9]

In America

The first distinctively American version of the 1662 prayer book was created in 1786 by Samuel Seabury, William White, and William Smith. One interesting feature of this version is that it brought together the best of the English prayer book with the Scottish one. (Scotland has had a special place in the hearts of the Episcopal Church; it was the Scottish church that ordained Samuel Seabury the first Episcopal bishop.) Some of the features of the liturgy highlighted in this book (for example, the offering of the bread and wine, which the Holy Spirit sanctifies) come from the Scottish liturgy, which ultimately derived from Eastern liturgies.

In 1789, the American prayer book was officially adopted. This was the first time that a church made liturgical decisions independently of political and secular authorities. Here was a distinctive emphasis of Episcopal polity. After the normal resistance, the new prayer book became the norm for over a hundred years. It was not until 1892 that the prayer book was revised. This version was less successful, so it was revised again in 1928.

The prayer book used in this chapter was first published in 1979. This prayer book benefited from the dramatic winds of change that came out of the Second Vatican Council in the Roman Catholic Church. Translations of certain prayers were agreed upon, and several major liturgical texts were discovered and incorporated. This revised prayer book provided a version of the service that was not dependent on Elizabethan English (it was no longer obligatory to use "thee" and "thy"). Instead of private baptism, the prayer book encouraged full participation in the regular worship service.

Perhaps the most important change is that the Holy Eucharist became the main service for Sunday. Morning Prayer was the practice of many churches prior to 1979. This is not surprising. The American church had become accustomed to a lack of clergy, which meant it had a strong laity. This combination made Morning Prayer very popular. However, as this book demonstrates, the Holy Eucharist is a real resource for the healthy and authentic living project. If the practice of breaking the bread in the book of Acts was daily, then taking the Eucharist once a week seemed like the minimum participation.

So to sum up this brief historical survey, there are three Liturgical Life Principles embedded in the history of the prayer book:

Liturgical Life Principle 29: We are joining a chain of countless individuals who have participated in and formed the liturgy before us; by it God has transformed our lives.

When you join an Episcopal Church service, you are joining to a family that reaches back in time to the Bible and is present throughout the world. God has been using this liturgy to change countless lives; every problem that we can imagine has been confronted by God in this liturgy. This means that we are forbidden to despair: what God has done for others, God can do for you.

Liturgical Life Principle 30: There was a tragic period in the life of the church when lay people were effectively excluded from the rich resources of the Holy Eucharist. We should therefore treasure and appreciate the gift of the sacrament.

Historical sensitivity makes us aware of how fortunate we are. We saw how the church took a wrong turn in the Middle Ages and effectively excluded lay people from the Eucharist. The church has now recovered a more biblical sense of the sacraments — to which all baptized Christians are invited. It is tragic when Christians exclude themselves from this precious gift that God is making available for the healthy and authentic living project.

Liturgical Life Principle 31: We should participate in the Eucharist at least once a week.

The revised Book of Common Prayer of 1979 made the Holy Eucharist the primary service on Sundays. And it really helps. It can make a difference in how we feel and look at the world. It is the most important part of the healthy and authentic living project.

Chapter Seven

The Power of Music and Symbol

It is often said that we never leave church humming the words to a sermon. It is the music that stays with us as we embark on the healthy and authentic living project. A vitally important part of the worship experience is the music.

In a typical Episcopal service, we can expect to sing three or four hymns. Most of them are taken from the Hymnal 1982, which is the Episcopal hymn book, a revision of the Hymnal 1940. The compilers were very imaginative on a number of levels. They reached out to a range of different traditions: they included hymns (and tunes) from Native American, African American, Hispanic, and Asian traditions. They ensured that there are hymns for the different moods of the church year, as well as for different types of services — Baptism, Eucharist, Confirmation, Marriage, Funerals, Ordination, Consecration of a Church, and Christian Life. Under the category "National Songs," we find the "National Anthem" and "America the Beautiful." At the back of the hymnal, we find the acknowledgments (copyright holders, authors, composers, etc.). From this, we discover that, for example, Charles Wesley (the inspiration behind Methodism) is the author of twenty-four hymns.

In addition to the Hymnal there are two other musical sources that are important. *Lift Every Voice and Sing II* is an African American hymnal. It was published in 1993, and, as it explains in the preface, it took music from a variety of sources: "Negro spirituals, traditional and contemporary Gospel songs, adapted Protestant hymns, missionary and evangelistic hymns and service music and mass settings in both traditional and Gospel settings."[10] The other source is *Wonder, Love and Praise,* which appeared in 1997. This was a supplement to the "Hymnal 1982," with hymn numbers helpfully starting where the "Hymnal 1982" left off, namely with hymn number 721. Many of the songs chosen for the supplement were already in widespread use in various congregations. It was primarily aimed at making sure that the Episcopal Church stayed current with musical trends.

Hymns and music can be an important part of the healthy and authentic living project. Some appreciation of the significance and origins of the hymns can help with this. And when this connection is made, it can stay with us in important ways.

Using Hymns in the Project

Liturgical Life Principle 32: We should connect with the narratives that birth the hymns and allow those narratives to impart grace to us.

Hymns come out of very contrasting settings. The connection with these settings can be significant. Two illustrations will suffice. Consider "There Is a Balm in Gilead" (#676). This beautifully haunting hymn invites us to enter into the world of the spirituals. It brings together the powerful biblical image of healing with the tragic reality of slavery. It is a positive answer to the question of Jeremiah (Jer. 8:22). Even though one feels discouraged and thinks one's work in vain, there is "a balm in Gilead to make the wounded whole." It is an amazing affirmation of faith emerging in the context of slavery. Colonial powers had determined that the most able of Africa should be turned into a commodity that can be bought and sold by whites. Torn from their families and communities in Africa, these individuals were trapped and chained in absurdly cramped quarters on slave ships. Sickness, sewage, and cruel brutality were their companions. Those who survived were auctioned to the rich to be property for the rest of their lives.

"There Is a Balm in Gilead" emerges from a setting of deep pain. It is a resistance song. Those who sing the words know that there are places where the pain will be ameliorated. It is deliberately ambiguous: on the one hand, the person singing the spiritual is invited to think of heaven; on the other hand, it is a reference to places elsewhere in the world where people live in freedom and the white people do not treat black people as property. So it is deliberately subversive. It is also a classic theological affirmation. As James Cone explains:

The idea of heaven provided ways for black people to affirm their humanity when other people were attempting to define them as non-persons. It enabled blacks to say yes to their right to be free by affirming God's promise to the oppressed of the freedom to be.[11]

The spirituals are remarkable. Singing the spirituals is an invitation to link ourselves with the pain of the community resisting the attempts of those in power to humiliate. One marvels at the faith of this community. A paradox of faith is that those who have most reason to doubt God (both God's goodness and God's existence) are often the most committed. It is the faith of the Africans that helped them survive this degrading treatment. It was a privilege to be invited to sing the spirituals. And the spirituals can challenge us to reflect on our lives. If this community with the horrendous challenge of slavery can find faith, then let us also find the same faith to cope.

Another text originating in the slave trade period is "Amazing Grace" (#671), written by John Newton in the eighteenth century. He was a slave trader who in the middle of a storm decided to give his life to God. It was a moment of judgment. He knew that slave trade was evil. Yet God preserved him through the storm and allowed him to live to old age. He wrote the words of the song as a reflection on his life.

Most of us are haunted by our past. We all find ourselves behaving in ways that are damaging to others. Where John Newton was deeply incriminated in the evil trade of slavery, we have our own (hopefully) less dramatic forms of incrimination. So we connect with John Newton and share with him the forgiveness that God can impart.

The music of a service can stay with us during the week. In those moments when we are alone or struggling, it is often a hymn that can come to the rescue. The hymns abide deep inside and can be a powerful resource for the healthy and authentic living project.

Using Music in Personal Devotions

Liturgical Life Principle 33: Music and meditation are means of transcending the stress of daily living.

In chapter 5 we explored the important world of the daily office. The rhythm of personal devotions is the lifeblood of the Christian faith. Life can be stressful; we are so overwhelmingly busy and preoccupied. Finding some time at the beginning and end of the day to live reflectively is an important mechanism that can alleviate stress.

Using music during this time can be life-enhancing. Christian music (CDs, MP3s, cassettes, etc.) is an excellent resource. And there is Christian music for every musical taste. One popular vehicle is the music of the ecumenical center at Taizé in France. The community was founded in 1949 by Brother Roger in a part of France where the community had protected Jewish refugees from the Nazis. Although it is a Protestant community, it has always had good relationships with Roman Catholics. Young people from throughout the world make their way to Taizé. With so many languages represented, the music needs to be simple and powerful. Jacques Berthier created the modern Taizé style. Often the music makes use of Latin because it is foreign to everyone. This, coupled with the simplicity and the fact that there are only five vowel sounds in Latin (thereby making pronunciation easier), makes it a good universal language. By lighting a candle and listening to Taizé music, we can create a very powerful resource that helps us cope with the difficulties of everyday living.

Appreciating the Symbolism of a Church

Liturgical Life Principle 34: We should allow the message of the moment to be reinforced in a variety of ways.

We have already noted how posture is part of the power and movement of the service. Standing to pray is a mark of respect (naturally if it is physically difficult to stand, then one should sit). There are many other ways in which the message of the moment can be reinforced. Color, for example, is one.

As we move through the different seasons of the Church, the color changes. White is used for Easter and Christmas. These are services of particular joy and festivity. Red is used for occasions associated with the martyrs and with the Holy Spirit. Purple is used for those periods when we should be penitent, and green is used for the rest of the year. The mood is partly set by the change of color.

In Episcopal churches, individuals often make the sign of the cross on themselves. Starting with the right hand on the forehead, the hand moves to the middle of the chest and then touches the left shoulder and then the right before returning to the center of the chest. This practice has been part of Christian piety for centuries. On one level, it is simply a recognition that as Christians we live under the redeeming power of the cross. It is a tactile reinforcement of the central message of Christianity.[12] Yet there are other interpretations. Some link the sign of the cross with the moment in our baptism when we are signed by the cross and sealed as "Christ's own forever." Others suggest that the signing of the cross is a prayer: God be in my head, God be in my heart, and God be in everything I do.

Different people sign the cross at different times in the service. Most do it when they receive the blessings from the priest. As the priest makes the sign of the cross, so the people receive that blessing by signing themselves. Some make the sign during the Creed when we reaffirm our confidence in the life to come. Yet others make the sign during the Benedictus (LLP 14 on page 62). These were the acclamations of the crowd as Jesus entered Jerusalem on Palm Sunday; a week later the crowd wanted him dead. To mark this association, many Christians make the sign of the cross at that point.

At various times in the year, incense might be used. Incense has associations with purity: we are invited to be purified as the incense rises to the sky. It is often used at certain important moments in the service, for example, immediately prior to the reading of the Gospel.

The idea here is that worship should involve all the senses. It is not simply a hearing or speaking or singing experience; it also involves posture, smell, and touch. We are encouraged in Romans 12 to offer "our bodies as a holy and acceptable sacrifice to God" (Rom. 12:1). To symbolize this offering to God we are encouraged to use all our senses in the worship of God.

With the symbolism, the attire, the colors, the setting, the words, and the movement, worship becomes a beautiful drama in which we all are invited to participate. Episcopal liturgy should always be done well: it has the capacity to take a congregation into the very presence of God.

An Instructed Eucharist

*For a Congregation to Understand
What Is Going On*

From time to time, it is helpful for a congregation to be taken through an "instructed Eucharist." This is especially important for those who are new to the community; however, it is often much appreciated also by those who have been coming for many years. There are a variety of ways of doing an instructed Eucharist. The approach suggested here involves the following. First, start by explaining to the congregation that the sermon will be replaced with short presentations during the service. These presentations will explain the significance of what follows in the service. Second, copy and distribute this appendix. This will not simply aid understanding; but it also means that members of the congregation can take it home and refer to it later. Third, you can choose anyone to be a reader (and have as many readers as you desire), but I do suggest that you find people who can read well in public.

Prior to the procession, the following is read:

Good morning. We are delighted that you are worshiping with us this morning. If you are new here, we give you a special welcome. We are delighted that you are with us. What follows is an experience of worship in the Episcopal tradition. You are being invited to participate in some "work" (this is the literal meaning of the word "liturgy": it is the work of the people). We are going to worship the Creator of everything that is — the God who made the countless planets and solar systems in our cosmos. And as we worship God, we are going to invite God to change us. We are going to give God some space in our lives to make a difference, to transform us into the persons that God always intended us to be.

In a moment the procession will start. In Episcopal churches, our posture is part of our participation. So I invite you to stand for the opening hymn and the procession of the clergy into the church. We stand out of respect, and you might want to bow as the cross passes you. The central symbol of our faith is the cross. In this symbol of state execution, we see the presence of God entering into suffering, identifying with it, and transforming it.

Once we are all present, the priest will invite us to participate in the opening acclamation. This moment in the service gives a sense of where we are in the church calendar. It is followed by the collect (prayer) for purity. In this prayer, we ask God to help us focus so that God can work in our lives. We now stand for the opening hymn.

Prior to the Gloria, the following is read:

Now we continue the gathering ritual with a hymn of praise (which is normally the Gloria, Kyrie, or Trisagion). Much of this service will be spent in the worship of God: so this opening hymn of praise is an appropriate part of our preparation. Worship is an opportunity for us to recognize in God the values of love, goodness, and justice and compare our lives with those values. As we acknowledge the nature of God and that God is worthy of praise, we are invited to think a little about the values in our lives. This is a theme we will return to at other times in the service.

After the Gloria, the priest will invite us to participate in the collect for the day. Please notice the greeting, "the Lord be with you" to which we all reply, "and also with you." As we encounter each other, we pray and trust that the Lord God Almighty will be present in our endeavors. This special prayer brings together the particular themes important for this Sunday.

Prior to the First Lesson, the following is read:

Given that this universe is so vast, it is difficult to see how we can know what God is like. So at this point in the service, we will be invited to learn about the nature of God. Through Scripture and the Eternal Word made flesh God has been revealed to us. Through the reading of Scripture we learn about a God who has encountered humanity with love and is calling for us to resist sin and live our full potential. Normally there is a lesson from the Old Testament (the Scriptures of the Jewish people), followed by a psalm (an ancient hymn), then an epistle or reading from the book of Acts, culminating in the reading of the Gospel.

Each reading contributes to the picture of how God relates to humanity. From the Old Testament, we learn how God has been revealed within Judaism. The psalms invite us to recognize our different moods — from rage to jealousy as well as praise and joy; as we sing or say the psalm we are invited to trust that God understands those moments when we are bewildered, as well as those when we are happy. This practice of using a psalm after the Old Testament reading goes back to the middle of the fourth century. The epistle (which means "letter") helps us discover the impact of Christ on the early Church. And the Gospel is the moment when we are invited to see in the life, death, and resurrection of Jesus the Eternal Word of God made manifest.

Once again our posture is symbolic. As the Gospel is read, we face the deacon or priest who is reading it. Often the Gospel is read from the middle of the congregation, thereby symbolizing the good news (which is the literal meaning of the word "Gospel") that has come into our midst.

After hearing about the Eternal Word (which is Jesus Christ) as disclosed in the Written Word (which is the Bible), we are now ready for the proclaimed word (which is the sermon). On this occasion, this instructed Eucharist is the sermon.

After the Gospel and before the Creed, the following is read:

Now that we know about the nature of the God we are worshiping, we are invited to stand and reaffirm our faith in the words of the creed. A creed is a statement of the Church's belief. The one used here is the creed formulated at the Council of Nicaea in 325 C.E. It tells the story of the Holy Trinity revealed in the life, death, and resurrection of Jesus of Nazareth.

Confident that the God revealed to humanity wants to hear from us, we can come into God's presence with our prayers. When we are in the presence of any important dignitary, we stand up or kneel. Given that God is supremely important, we will either stand or kneel. At this point we pray together for the Church and the world. Many of us are in Church this morning with problems. Please offer your problems to God and, at the same time, locate your problems in the context of a world that has many problems.

Our prayers will flow into confession. Every week we are invited back to bow the knee and acknowledge we have messed up. Most of us struggle with areas that are a particular challenge to us. If we confess with sincerity and a real desire for repentance, then God will forgive us. And we can face a new week, drawing on the resources of God, to work harder on those areas that we find difficult.

So let us now stand and reaffirm our faith in the words of the Creed.

Prior to the Peace, the following is read:

This is the point in the service where we move from the Word to Holy Communion. We are first going to pass the peace — an ancient Christian practice suggested by St. Paul in 1 Corinthians 16:20. Being at peace with each other is a Christian obligation. We are invited to be at "peace" not simply with those around us, but also with all those we have encountered in the last week. We should use this opportunity to resolve to work harder to be at peace with those we find difficult. In addition, it is important to bring the peace of the Lord to all those in our past who hurt us. It is so easy for us to live with unresolved hurt: in the symbolism of touching the hands of others you are invited to release the pain and hurt that is part of the past. This moment of peacemaking comes immediately before the offertory (the moment when we give of ourselves to God). Jesus instructs us to make sure we are at peace with those around us before bringing our gifts to God (Matt. 5:23–24).

After shaking hands, the priest will take a sentence from Scripture and invite us to offer back to God what God has so generously given us. God has given us time, talents, and treasures, which we should give back to God. It is an opportunity to make sure that we are not allowing "things" to dominate our lives. It is an opportunity to reflect on what we are doing for God.

Prior to the Great Thanksgiving, the following is read:

Now we are being invited to the table. The prayer that the priest will read is called the "Great Thanksgiving" — the word "Eucharist" literally means thanksgiving. We are going to reflect on everything that God has done for us. We are going to be invited to respond with gratitude for the love and grace that God has bestowed on humanity. This prayer starts with the "Sursum Corda" (literally, lift up your hearts). This dialogue between the priest and the people continues through the prayer. There are two other moments when the people break in: first, the Sanctus (holy), where we join the distinguished company of heaven and sing praise to God; and second, the memorial acclamation, where we remember the saving work of Christ.

The prayer moves dramatically from a sense of gratitude for creation, the incarnation, and the redemption made possible by Christ. When it comes to the words of institution, we remember the act of love in which Christ gave himself for us. And at the epiclesis (which means "invocation"), the priest asks the Father (the Creator of everything that is) to send the Holy Spirit (the aspect of God that makes God present to us now) to enable the Divine Word (the son) to interpenetrate the elements of bread and wine so that they are to us the "body and blood of Christ." This is a miracle. God is providing us with a resource to enable us to live differently — to live as God intended.

Out of joy and without fear we can utter the prayer that Jesus taught his disciples. Then the priest breaks the consecrated bread, a symbol of how brokenness can be the key to life. Then we can come forward to receive.

To receive the bread and wine, you should kneel (if you are able) at the rail. With one hand supporting the other, you receive the bread. And then you have a choice: you can either dip the bread into the wine or eat the bread and drink the wine separately. (You may also just receive the bread and then leave the rail.) If you would rather not receive, the act of placing your hands across your chest will invite the priest to bless you.

God has given us the gift of the Holy Communion. We share this feast and leave the Table with our hearts and lives ready to serve God for another week.

Prior to the Postcommunion prayer, the following is read:

We are now coming to the end of this service of thanksgiving. In this prayer, we bring the themes of the service together and prepare for another week of service in God's world. The priest will send us out with a blessing — a practice that was included in the 1549 prayer book. And the priest or the deacon will dismiss us — sending us to live transformed lives of grace and love in the world.

Appendix Two

Liturgy and Transformation

For the Scholar

This is a reading of the liturgy. It is an attempt to take the historic purpose of the liturgy — namely, the worship of God — and unpack its effectiveness in creating faithful disciples of our Lord. A central claim being made in this book is that liturgy makes a difference to life.

The constructive connection between Christianity and life has been central to the ministry of Robert Schuller. Schuller was a disciple of Norman Vincent Peale (1898–1993). Peale was the author of *The Power of Positive Thinking,* which exhorted readers to use a variety of techniques to absorb the power of God in one's life and exclude all negativity. Although Schuller shares with Peale the idea that the Christian story can help individuals to live better and more constructive lives, it is carefully grounded in traditional evangelical beliefs.

Schuller founded the Garden Grove Community Church in California, which in 1980 became the Crystal Cathedral. Its purpose is to provide stress-filled Americans with a message of hope. On his website, which explains the beliefs of the "hope-building heart of Crystal Cathedral Ministries," Schuller tells his story. He wanted to challenge the perception of Christianity as the religion of the "do nots." Schuller explains:

> God called me to be a missionary to un-churched persons in the middle of the twentieth century. I quickly discovered that the non-religious people turned off religion when I talked about "sins of commission . . ." I came to a conclusion that sin is caused by "lack of faith" in God and His ways. So my God-given mission became to build faith in the minds of doubters.

We must ask the question, "What does God want me to do?" It is not enough just to have peace of mind knowing that in Christ we are forgiven, that our guilt is gone. But we also need to leave church with a God-given dream. It is time to focus more on the sins of omission, to listen to the dreams that God sends into our imagination. For not to listen to them and not to try to turn them into achievements, could be the worst sin many people will ever commit.[13]

Schuller insists that the focus of the Christian drama is as much on the realization of our God-given human potential as it is on the recognition that God has redeemed us. For Schuller, it is a sin to deny the potential that God has made possible. It has been a message with significant appeal. There are ten thousand members of the Crystal Cathedral and the television show *The Hour of Power* reaches millions.

Schuller has been a major inspiration and influence on others in the megachurch movement. Two illustrations will suffice. Rick Warren (born 1954) is the pastor of Saddleback Church in Lake Forest, California. This is a church that has twenty-two thousand participants in its service every week. His *Purpose Driven Life* has sold over 25 million copies. Like Schuller's message, it is an invitation for men and women to get their lives sorted out. In the *Purpose Driven Life*, the process takes forty days.

Another illustration is Joel Osteen (born 1963). Osteen's church in Texas was founded by his father, John Osteen. John Osteen died in 1999, and Joel took over. As with Schuller and Warren, Osteen offers a statement of beliefs that is clearly and explicitly evangelical. However, he adds a final affirmation, where he writes: "We believe as children of God, we are overcomers and more than conquerors and God intends for each of us to experience the abundant life He has in store for us."[14]

This theme, that the life that has been saved should be hopeful, full, and rich, pervades Osteen's books. His first book, in 2004 was called *Your Best Life Now*; his second was *Become a Better You*. Both have been phenomenally successful.

It is the assumption of this reading of the liturgy that Schuller et al. have a point. No Episcopalian should be nervous about recognizing that God wants lives changed through worship. Indeed our nervousness about associating ourselves with this insight is a key part of the weakness of the mainline churches. The work of the liturgy has always been life-transforming. But with the mega-churches making this connection explicit, the mainline has — in a rather extraordinary way — denied it. Indeed Schuller has been the object of derision and criticism. According to the critics, a gospel of positive thinking and prosperity is a distortion of the Gospel.

Schuller is actually much more nuanced than his critics give him credit for. And Rick Warren is uncompromising: for him there is no incompatibility between witnessing to the transformation that God is making available to every human being and taking social issues seriously. Warren is an increasingly prominent advocate for environmental issues. He has called for resources to alleviate the AIDS epidemic in Africa and to stop the genocide in Darfur. But even if Schuller goes to an extreme, it is wrong for the mainline, in reaction, to ignore the transformation of lives made possible by the Gospel.

This book has explored some twenty contrasting messages embedded in the one service, which make a range of demands on our lives. Every week we are called to reflect on our priorities, our attitude toward possessions, our need to seek forgiveness, and our responsibility for coming to peace with our past. It is a rich and demanding process. It is also comprehensive. The temptation for the megachurch is to focus on the message of reassurance, so that the challenge of justice is played down. The Episcopal liturgy will not let you evade the total challenge of the Gospel.

The total challenge is realized in a variety of ways. One is the challenge of the lectionary. The lectionary is an ecumenical project that works systematically through Scripture over a three-year period. It means that over this period we will hear and reflect on a full range of biblical themes. In Year A, for example, we work through the Gospel of Luke. As a result, the warning against riches and our obligations to the poor are highlighted week after week. Episcopalians cannot simply enjoy the reassuring message of hope; they are obligated to engage with the difficult and hard words of challenge.

Although I recognize Schuller's achievement in emphasizing the transforming message of the Gospel, it is also true that I recognize that the Gospel can be truncated. It can end up being all reassurance and no challenge, all resurrection and no taking up the cross, all love and no justice. The Episcopal liturgy brings it all together. There is plenty of reassurance, resurrection, and love, but also challenge, cross, and justice.

In bringing it all together, the Episcopal liturgy provides both health and authenticity. We looked at the meaning of these terms in the introduction. It is worth revisiting the points made there and comparing them with Schuller's approach. The focus of Schuller et al. is on health, creating a positive outlook for living in the world. This is good and definitely a component of the Episcopal liturgy. However, this project is larger: it also invites authenticity. As noted in the introduction, the difference is that a healthy disposition is not necessarily authentic. We don't want a contrived positive outlook, we don't want to ignore the triggers that are so damaging, and we do want to face up to the hurt in our lives. Authenticity requires that we deal with these issues.

It is the argument of this book that authenticity should underpin and sustain the healthy disposition. Again as we saw in the intro-duction, authenticity can create many paradoxes. It is authentic to live life aware of the reality of death. As a result, when illness fi-nally strikes, one has a much healthier attitude toward that illness. Schuller might well affirm the appropriateness of this connection; the theme of living life in the light of death, however, is not promi-nent in his ministry or writings. Precisely because of the centrality of the Eucharist, this connection is inescapable in the Episcopal lit-urgy. The goal of the Episcopal liturgy is to provide a framework in which every context can be accommodated — from the struggle of the Christian dalits in India to the busy businessman on Wall Street.

The assertion that the goal of the Episcopal liturgy is to pro-vide a framework in which all people (and their complex lives) can be accommodated will be hotly contested. So in the concluding pages of this book, I shall briefly identify and respond to the various objections to the project explored in this book.

Objections and Replies

The first and primary objection will come from those who insist that the sole purpose of worship is to worship God. It is not for us. It is the creature acknowledging our place in creation. Any semi-psychological use of the liturgy, according to this objection, is a distortion of the purpose of liturgy.

The sustained discussion of the importance of worship in chapter 3 responds to this objection. Let me reiterate. It is certainly true that in worshiping God we recognize our dependence and our connection with the transcendent. We orient ourselves appropriately. Let me add that there is a sense in which God enjoys the worship of the people of God. It represents a rightly ordered creation recognizing the beauty and love of the Creator. However, recognition of the privilege of worship is not incompatible with the insight that worship does us a world of good. It orients us to ensure that our priorities are appropriately adjusted. As I argued in chapters 1 and 3, worship is the mechanism by which we discern what is morally good. It is the objective standard outside us that helps us to know what is right and good.

As God enjoys the worship of God's people, so we learn to enjoy the worship of God. As we discover the love of God, so we discover our core connection with the reality that underpins everything that is. We find ourselves transformed toward healthy and authentic living.

Worship of God is accompanied by the obligation to confess our sin, to be at peace with our neighbor, and to give of our resources to God. These aspects of the worship service are all aimed at adjusting our view of the world. They help transform us into better people. All these features are embedded in the traditional service. Therefore the objection that worship is for God and not for us is not sustained.

A second objection is that the entire project is not biblical, and perhaps the lack of explicit references to Scripture in chapters 1 through 5 might be cited as evidence. However, to raise this objection is to misunderstand the entire project. The services described are deeply biblical. It has been estimated that 80 percent of the prayer book is derived from the Bible.[15] The proper way to understand the project is to see it as part of the process of sanctification. Indeed the author of 2 Peter captures the essence of the project in the description at the beginning of that book:

> His divine power has given us everything we need for life and godliness through our knowledge of him who called us by his own glory and goodness. Through these he has given us his very great and precious promises, so that through them you may participate in the divine nature and escape the corruption in the world caused by evil desires. For this very

reason, make every effort to add to your faith goodness; and to goodness, knowledge; and to knowledge, self-control; and to self-control, perseverance; and to perseverance, godliness; and to godliness, brotherly kindness; and to brotherly kindness, love. For if you possess these qualities in increasing measure, they will keep you from being ineffective and unproductive in your knowledge of our Lord Jesus Christ. But if anyone does not have them, he is near-sighted and blind, and has forgotten that he has been cleansed from his past sins.

(2 Pet. 1:3–9, NIV)

The picture in Peter is that we need to make "every effort to add" to our faith certain qualities that start with goodness and move to love. On the way we should master "self-control" and "perseverance." This short epistle sees us "growing into faith," or, as the language of the first epistle puts it, "Like newborn babies, crave pure spiritual milk, so that by it you may grow up in your salvation" (1 Pet. 2:2).

There are plenty of other passages in Scripture that encourage us to recognize the work of holiness that we are called to realize. The Gospels call us to imitate the words and deeds of Jesus (see Acts 1:1). Paul encourages an attitude toward suffering that recognizes the way in which "suffering produces perseverance; perseverance, character; and character hope" (Rom. 5:3–5). In the next chapter, Paul warns against the attitude that invites us to sin more "so that grace may increase" (Rom. 6:1). Instead, he instructs his readers to "not let sin reign in your mortal body so that you obey its evil desires. Do not offer the parts of your body to sin, as instruments of wickedness, but rather offer yourself to God, to those who have been brought from death to life; and offer the parts of your body to him as instruments of righteousness" (Rom. 6:12–13). Paul invites us to live the transformed life made possible by the Gospel. We are invited to see that God wants to make us as God always intended. The argument of this book is deeply biblical.

A third objection is that the megachurches are a corruption of true Christianity and that this book takes a line much too positive toward their pastors. In the end, this argument is based primarily on prejudice and not on data. Indeed the data from those who study megachurches indicates that these communities are good, strong, and successful at encouraging the spiritual life of their members. Scott Thumma, the sociologist of religion who has done much work on megachurches, says that his findings show that the most significant factor in the growth of the megachurches is the quality of the worship:

> The worship is perceived as exciting and informal, the attendees feel optimistic about the church's future because it is growing and successful, and their spiritual lives are fulfilling as they learn and act out their faith in ministry. These multiple dimensions of the committed attendee's intense satisfaction with the church create such excitement in them that they want to tell others; they are highly motivated to engage in active recruitment out of an intense desire to express this excitement and satisfaction. They want to share the good news about the church and about what God is doing in their lives.[16]

Instead of arguing that the megachurches are a vehicle for distorted Christianity, I am arguing that we need to take seriously the discovery they have made. But I am also pushing back and suggesting that the spirit of life-transformation, so highlighted by Schuller et al., is already available in the rich liturgical life of the Anglican tradition, which has been doing this work for centuries. Most members know this already. Our clergy and leadership have known it less well — or if they know they have not dared to make the connection for fear of being linked with the Schullers of this world.

The time has come for the Episcopal Church to explain that our liturgy is intended to provide hope when hopelessness seems to be the only option. It is intended to enable us to cope when coping is difficult. It is intended to help us confront the demons of our past when we imagine that the demons are bound to triumph.

Episcopalians need to be willing to explain ourselves much more clearly. We need to educate our congregations much more effectively. We need to invite people to join the work of the liturgy and grow to love it. Every Episcopal church should set a goal of growing bigger because there are people out there who need the rich resource of the liturgy. There are so many damaged lives that need to be shaped by our liturgical tradition. We owe it to them to let them know. We owe it to God to let them know.

Notes

1. See Timothy Egan, "Wall Street Meets Pornography," *New York Times,* October 23, 2000.

2. See Joan D. Atwood and Limor Schwartz, M.A., "Cyber-Sex: The New Affair Treatment Considerations," *Journal of Couple and Relationship Therapy* 1, no. 3 (2002): 37–56.

3. C. S. Lewis, *Letters to Malcolm: Chiefly on Prayer* (London: Geoffrey Bles, 1964), 12.

4. I am grateful to my younger brother, Michael Markham, for this description of church.

5. Rush Rhees, *Without Answers* (London: Routledge and Kegan Paul 1969), 113.

6. Sometimes people kneel for the prayers. The action of kneeling represents reverence and penitence.

7. Keith Ward, *Divine Action* (London: Collins, 1990), 165–66.

8. For sacred space see *www.sacredspace.ie.*

9. I am grateful to Dr. Larry Golemon, who made this point as part of the Ecumenical Project at Virginia Theological Seminary.

10. *Lift Every Voice and Sing II,* Preface, viii.

11. James H. Cone, *The Spirituals and the Blues* (Maryknoll, N.Y.: Orbis Books, 2001), 82. Cone is nervous about making too much of the "political ambiguity," although he does concede that "heaven had its this-worldly topographical referents" (81).

12. I am grateful for a conversation with Tom Kryder-Reid for this section.

13. See Robert Schuller at *www.crystalcathedral.org.*

14. See Joel Osteen at *www.lakewood.cc.*

15. See Sue Careless, *Discovering the Book of Common Prayer: A Hands-On Approach,* vol. 1: *Daily Prayer* (Toronto: ABC Publishing 2003), 26.

16. Scott Thumma and Dave Travis, *Beyond Megachurch Myths: What We Can Learn from America's Largest Churches* (San Francisco: Jossey-Bass, 2007), 158.

Additional Resources

Black, Vicki K. *Welcome to the Church Year: An Introduction to the Seasons of the Episcopal Church.* Harrisburg, Pa.: Morehouse Publishing, 2004. This is a delightful introduction to the beauty of the Church year. All the symbolism of color and movement of the calendar is described very clearly.

Hatchett, Marion J. *Commentary on the American Prayer Book.* San Francisco: HarperSanFrancisco, 1995. The classic commentary on the prayer book, which gives a detailed history on every prayer and element of all the services. A substantial reference work.

Markham, Ian. *Understanding Christian Doctrine.* Oxford: Blackwell Publishing, 2008. This is intended as an accessible introduction to the major themes of the Christian faith — the nature of God, reasons for belief, the Trinity, the Incarnation, Atonement, and life after death.

Prichard, Robert. *A History of the Episcopal Church.* Harrisburg, Pa.: Morehouse Publishing, 1999. For those frustrated with the brevity of the historical section in this book, this is an outstanding history of the Episcopal Church. Clear and accurate, it is a complete delight.

Ward, Keith. *Divine Action.* London: Flame, Collins, 1990. For those with questions about prayer and divine action, this is an excellent study. This is not for beginners; it is fairly technical.

Ward, Keith. *God: A Guide for the Perplexed.* Oxford: Oneworld, 2002. For those who would like some additional help with an understanding of God, this is an excellent study.

Webber, Christopher. *A User's Guide to the Holy Eucharist Rites I and II.* Harrisburg, Pa.: Morehouse Publishing, 1997. For those who would like to compare my reading with a more traditional reading, this is the perfect book.

Webber, Christopher. *Welcome to the Episcopal Church: An Introduction to Its History, Faith, and Worship.* Harrisburg, Pa.: Morehouse Publishing, 1999. This is an accurate and delightfully brief survey of the history and life of the Episcopal Church.